THE APPLES
IN STEREO

ALSO AVAILABLE

THE APPLES IN STEREO

Josh Bloom

**J-Card
Press**

ISBN: 979-8-9917394-2-9 (print)
ISBN: 979-8-9917394-3-6 (ebook)

Library of Congress Control Number: 2025947176

J-Card Press
460 Center Street #6578
Moraga, California 94570

Designed by Catherine O'Leary

www.jcardpress.com

This book is dedicated to the memory of Ken Shopsin. You didn't kick me out of the restaurant. You took me in.

You exclaimed, "When you first meet Josh, he's kind of an asshole, but when you get to know him, he's a really nice guy!" I repeat this story often.

You kicked a dude I was dating out of your hospital room, but not until after insisting he was lucky to have met me.

That was the last time I saw you. I regret not coming into the shop early to accept your offer of teaching me the best way to fry chicken cutlets.

CONTENTS

1. HEARING THE SONGS OVER THE SOUND OF THE SCENE: ROBERT HAD TOO MUCH TO DO!

This book is not about the Elephant 6 Recording Company, so let's talk about it. Beginning with its rise to recognition in the mid-nineties and rocking right on through to this very moment, the Athens, Georgia, and Denver, Colorado–based music and art collective called the Elephant 6 Recording Co. has been extensively documented, especially considering it was (or is?) a relatively small and only moderately maintained cultural movement compared to the size of its impact.

"Was" or "is" represents the looseness of it all that was or is (you get it!) an essential part of the collective's winning charm. Even with the collision of the many gleefully disorganized agendas of the members that led to its fragmentation, the ragtag vibe of Elephant 6, and how that aesthetic permeated the music, is what powers ongoing discussion in books, in films, and on social media decades beyond the heyday of the collective.

It's happening right now!

Before Elephant 6 even existed in name, the existing mythology suggests it was conjured from the ether by Robert Schneider, Will Hart, Bill Doss, and Jeff Mangum, friends since childhood living in and around Ruston, Louisiana. As it developed, the collective became anchored by its core (here come the apple puns!) bands, the Olivia Tremor Control (Will and Bill), Neutral Milk Hotel (Jeff), and the Apples in Stereo (Robert).

Robert was eventually seen as the collective's de facto leader. In addition to the roles he brought to his own band, the Apples in Stereo, Robert produced, engineered, composed, and performed on records by the Olivia Tremor Control, Neutral Milk Hotel, and eventually, many others.

Robert had too much to do!

This situation was made even more challenging by the fact that the Apples, and Robert's studio Pet Sounds, were in Denver, far away from Athens, where the camaraderie, community, and communication of the rest of the collective created the key element to defining the mystique and subsequent media buzz around Elephant 6.

In 2010, seventeen years removed from the band's debut EP, the Apples in Stereo were on the precipice of a major commercial breakthrough when what turned out to be their final album (for now?) was released.

The Apples in Stereo has historically been covered and discussed in the context of the collective.

If the band had formed autonomously, as bands typically do, would it still be active today? Their song "Energy," objectively the biggest single by the Apples, was released in 2007. Perhaps the band would have found mainstream success in their third decade independent of the Elephant 6 Recording Co.?

I have known Robert for thirty years. He knows me to be fair and fairly candid. I made it clear to him at the outset of this project that I was not ghostwriting a memoir. Robert tells me that he doesn't see writing a memoir on his horizon. I understand why. It would be a painful endeavor at this point in his life. Robert says that the most important part of making music is friendship. He has suffered the loss of too many friends, too soon.

This particular book about the Apples in Stereo is meant to draw you closer to the songs, the sensitivity in the songwriting, and stories of the songwriters.

In the context of Elephant 6, the Apples are consistently perceived as the "pop" band, never receiving the credit for how emotionally substantial their material and the performances of it are. The Olivia Tremor Control is "art," Neutral Milk Hotel is "deep," the Apples in Stereo is "pop," and that's that.

Let's overturn the marketing myth for the sake of rock history!

"Thank you for noticing," Robert says, adding, in a way that tends to unnecessarily, and often to his detriment, subtly self-cancel credit for his artistic accomplishments. "It's also less artistic to talk about how artistic you are."

Okay, fine. I'll do it for you.

Robert may feel that he has already said everything he has to say through his work. Robert is the only one who can truly capture Robert. I hope he writes that memoir someday.

When it comes to Robert's role as the leader of Elephant 6, I humorously hold an image of him in my mind as "the Principal," summoning artists across the country from Athens to Denver to record at Pet Sounds, which I imagine as the "Principal's Office."

Robert was in charge, but in reality Pet Sounds was

no office, existing in a dilapidated building that probably should have been condemned, and soon was. During the brief period that it existed, so many songs that mean so much to so many people were written and recorded there.

The physically dark surroundings (my personal recollection of the place) represent the darkness in the Apples in Stereo catalog for me now, which may seem strange considering how the band is so known for their sunny songs when compared to the rest of the collective.

Let's take a new listen to these songs and try to hear them over the sound of the scene. No lingering history can outweigh the music contained on bulk reel-to-reel tape. The lines to read between are narrow, but the drama can be heard in the grooves.

When I began to write this book, I admitted to Robert that I had a preconceived bias against the final two Apples albums and planned to focus on the years when the band mainly consisted of Robert, Hilarie Sidney, John Hill, and Eric Allen. Robert and Hilarie were a couple during the period that contains the work I love the most, including their debut album, *Fun Trick Noisemaker* (released in 1995), through to *Velocity of Sound* (released in 2002).

Hilarie left the Apples in Stereo after recording but before the release of the band's penultimate album, *New Magnetic Wonder*, which came out in 2007, five years after *Velocity of Sound*. Hilarie's departure contributed to my bias against *New Magnetic Wonder* and the record that followed, 2010's *Travellers in Space and Time*.

Is my bias against these records reasonable? Maybe not, but when it comes to art, reason is no factor.

The records released during Hilarie's years with the Apples have only left more of an impression on me since, and Hilarie's prolific songwriting throughout the 2020s with her band the High Water Marks has also made me understand and revere her role in the Apples even more.

Time has proved the influence and permanence of the Hilarie era of Apples material, so I expected my conversations with Robert for this book would only serve to solidify my point of view about the later work. This is why what I call the "classic" configuration of the Apples in Stereo—John, Robert, Hilarie, and Eric—is pictured on the cover of this book.

Oh, wait, here's Robert: "In our band, my primary nickname is 'the Jet.' John Hill is strictly known as 'Fuzz,' and Eric is strictly known as 'PRE.' Hilarie was the source of nicknames—the oracle of good nicknames!"

Just for fun, I follow up with Hilarie about this, and while I was not able to confirm if she had an Apples nickname herself, my back-and-forth with Robert reveals more of the narrative about the Hilarie era of the Apples.

"John was roommates with Hilarie before I met him," Robert says.

I ask if Hilarie also knew Eric Allen before he joined the Apples.

"Yes! She brought them both into the band," Robert replies.

I lean into it: "So, Hilarie basically put the Apples together?"

"She certainly put the second version together!"

"THE version," I reply, all-caps included.

Robert does not respond.

To clarify, the "first version," as opposed to the "second version" of the Apples, was formed in 1992 and included bassist Jim McIntyre, guitarist Chris Parfitt, Robert, and Hilarie.

"When I met Robert and he said he was forming a band and he needed a drummer, I was persistent in saying, 'I'll be the drummer,'" Hilarie says. "It didn't matter that I had never really played the drums."

"Someone who is not trained in drums first makes the best drummer, in my opinion, and she started as a guitar player," Robert explains before enthusing, "Hilarie is the greatest drummer in rock music!"

John Hill permanently replaced Parfitt in 1994. Jeff Mangum of Neutral Milk Hotel briefly joined the band on bass following McIntyre's departure, also in 1994, before being permanently replaced by Eric Allen in 1995.

The contribution of Hilarie (nickname unknown) as part of the Apples in Stereo with her bandmates the Jet, Fuzz, and PRE during her fourteen-year run is essential. Not only in the context of this particular band's musical legacy, but also as a key piece of Elephant 6, a cultural touchstone that continues to be extensively documented and referenced decades later.

Her contribution is made all the more noteworthy by the fact that she was a woman navigating her earned place as the drummer in a late-nineties rock band during a time when prevailing attitudes toward women in bands were not as evolved as they are today (and when I say "as they are today," this may unfortunately mean something different depending on when and where you are reading this).

Hilarie is a founding member of both the Apples and Elephant 6, and the only woman who is a founding member of both. In those roles, and as an innovative lifelong songwriter and performer in her own right, Hilarie is currently the most prolific Elephant 6 artist, having released four full-length albums and counting with her band the

High Water Marks from 2020 to 2025.

She has been under-recognized at best and marginalized at worst.

Let's fix that!

Robert told me several times that he did not want to be the primary source for this book, which I did not believe, because when he would bring it up, it was during the course of many intense weeks of marathon texting at all hours of the day and night. He did not want to be the primary source while clearly being the primary source! I appreciate Robert's insistence on the equal contributions of his bandmates to the Apples, and I don't disagree, but Robert is the primary source (and primary sorcerer!) in the Apples in Stereo story. Still, as with any source, it is up to you to decide how prime the information really is.

When you know someone for a long time, you will eventually find their edges, and my dynamic with Robert resulted in a falling-out between us for a period of time that has ultimately served to make us better friends in the long run. Any intense person who has been through a breakup-makeup (personal or professional) with another intense person knows that the less agreeable sides you have seen are forgiven but not forgotten.

In our conversations I was fair, fairly candid, and sometimes nervous, especially around the sensitive topics of Robert's romantic and professional partnership with Hilarie, his working relationship with Jeff Mangum of Neutral Milk Hotel, and the ongoing pain of the untimely passing of his best friends, Bill Doss (in 2012) and Will Hart (just a few months prior to this writing, in late 2024).

Bill had joined the Apples as a touring member in 2006 and permanent member in 2010. Having his childhood friend on the road and in the band after Hilarie's departure was good for Robert, but his sense of stability was soon undermined.

"I had just gotten a fun fisheye filter for my Olympus!" Hilarie says of this Pet Sounds Recording Studio shot taken during the making of Music from the Unrealized Film Script: Dusk at Cubist Castle *by the Olivia Tremor Control. (L–R): Will Hart, John Fernandes, Robert Schneider, Bill Doss. Photo by Hilarie Sidney, courtesy of the Apples in Stereo.*

Robert says he devoted himself to his current career in mathematics "instantly" on the day Bill died (Robert is currently an assistant professor of mathematical sciences at Michigan Technological University). "I talked to him one day, and the next day he was dead. He had no health problems, nothing. It was out of nowhere," Robert told *Atlanta* magazine in 2018.

Then, another lifelong friend of Robert's passed not long after Will died.

"It feels like in *Back to the Future* when all the people are vanishing from the photograph," Robert told me about an actual high school photo he posted on Facebook of himself with his two friends.

Moments ago, on June 11, 2025, it was announced that Robert's musical hero, Brian Wilson of the Beach Boys, whom Robert had met several times, had also died. The Apples in Stereo song "Glowworm" from the band's debut album *Fun Trick Noisemaker* is about Brian.

Robert re-creates an iconic image of his musical hero, Brian Wilson, as seen tacked to the wall of Pet Sounds as inspiration. Hold your book or screen up to your face, and you will feel inspired by Brian too! Photo by Hilarie Sidney, courtesy of the Apples in Stereo.

"In the last year, almost everybody I was close to in Ruston passed away," Robert says. "I am a lonely survivor."

It is shocking and tragic to me that Robert has lost so many of the best friends that he forged his identity with, that he most identified with, and that the world most identifies him with, at such relatively young ages. Bill was just forty-three. Will was fifty-three.

Because Robert and I have a history as on-off-on-again friends, I can speak from personal experience to complete a picture of him as the more emotionally complex person, and therefore, songwriter, recording artist, and producer I know him to be. This is in contrast to how I have seen him portrayed in media coverage, books, and films about the Apples in Stereo and the Elephant 6 Recording Co. What this means for you is the potential to read more deeply into the songs that compose the Apples in Stereo catalog.

Brian Wilson inspires Robert in real life! This 2008 meeting with Brian in Nashville at the Ryman Auditorium is one of several times that Robert got to spend quality time with his musical hero. Photo by the late Roger Ferguson (father of Apples member John Ferguson).

Robert's unending enthusiasm for, and encouragement of, other artists is one of his most appealing attributes as a person, but it is also his Achilles heel as a promoter of his own work.

Let's fix that!

Is Robert's humility a remnant of the "no selling out" post-*Nevermind* mindset of the late nineties that saw artists grappling with how to maintain their authenticity amid the internet's increasing ability to allow audiences to peek behind the curtain of the marketing and money that went into making a band *appear* "authentic"?

Following Robert and Hilarie's divorce and Hilarie's eventual departure from the Apples in Stereo in 2006, Robert seemed to enter a phase of his career that I call "grabbing at the ring," which I will explain further in chapter 8.

In the specific case of the Apples, there is a literal ring!

The actor Elijah Wood is best known for his recurring role as Frodo in director Peter Jackson's *Lord of the Rings* films.

"I really like some of the films he was in prior to that too, like *The Ice Storm*," Robert adds.

Yes. That is a good one.

Elijah released the last two Apples albums—the two I still raise an eyebrow about—on what a skeptical, sometimes cynical, eyebrow-raising dude like me might call a "vanity" record label.

I don't take criticizing the involvement of a movie star in the band's career any further than the use of the word "vanity," however. I believe Elijah loves the Apples, because why wouldn't he?

I am not looking to pick fights in the shire!

Have I mentioned that I have a preconceived bias against this era of the Apples and the two albums associated with it? If you don't remember, you may be smoking pipe weed. This concludes my flurry of *Lord of the Rings* puns.

Fame—even proximity to fame—is intoxicating. It can

make artists "grab at the ring," especially when that panacea is tied into what you were passionately doing naturally when nobody was looking. It's even worse when you think you are smart and experienced enough to stay grounded as it happens.

Full transparency: Robert disagrees with me about "the ring."

"It didn't exist," he claims. "My bandmates are epic people, and my band had legendary adventures, and we carried a whole collective along with us. We refused to take the ring that was constantly dangled in front of us."

Regardless, it is my hope with this book that the entire Apples catalog will be discovered by new fans and evaluated anew by existing ones. In that spirit, I have been convinced through a powerful sales pitch by Robert to set an example by doing just that for the 2007 and 2010 albums *New Magnetic Wonder* and *Travellers in Space and Time*.

"*New Magnetic Wonder* achieves the vision of *Fun Trick Noisemaker*, and of Elephant 6," Robert says. "It reunified the collective at the time. I think it's our best album."

Big, if true!

My primary interest in the Elephant 6 Recording Co. has always been the fact that it managed to exist at all. I am fascinated with how a large group of people can convene and combine to form a sustained creative influence that is far greater and historically relevant than the sum of its parts.

In a group of artists aligned with a common purpose and goals, it is the individual artists whom I am most curious about. What motivates people to throw their lives in with others, and how do internal and external forces precipitate the erosion of those motivations?

"We live a lifestyle that is very romantic, off the grid,

and DIY," Robert says of this trajectory. "Starving artists are like shamans for the rest of society. They actually allow us to do drugs and abuse ourselves, even when they generally disapprove of the behavior. They almost want to see us go insane, and then relish the storyline."

What if the Apples in Stereo, a subset of this group of artists, was not a subset at all? Would Hilarie have received the recognition she deserved as a founding member and indispensable contributor to the success of both? Would the band's final two records still be their final two records, and would I harbor my preconceived bias against them?

Robert says, "It's weird for me, you know, because the collective itself is my greatest project. Founding the movement supersedes my own songwriting and even my own production vision. But my songwriting and my productions are my personal art form; that is where my soul is as an artist."

Robert and Hilarie are both in second marriages that have long outlasted the one that they shared. Maybe there is a second marriage for this version of the Apples, the version I lean into as "THE version." Even if this idea is only hypothetical for now, renewal is real, and it is not just for musicians. It is for music too.

2. THE NAME OF THIS BAND IS?

The Apples in Stereo or The Apples in stereo or The Apples In Stereo or The Apples (in stereo) or THE APPLES in stereo?

"It is 'The Apples in stereo,' officially, but I like to be vague and not nail it down in public," Robert explains. "In the last fifteen years or so, it has become common to call us 'Apples in Stereo,' without 'the,' which I kind of like too."

"We're The Apples, the music's in stereo," Robert said to a publication credited as a "College Magazine" by the *Houston Press* in its reprint of the quote. Robert was unable to recall the name of the publication when asked (sorry, "College Magazine"!). "It's not actually the band name—it's a step back from it, a band name once removed. We're The Apples, in stereo."

"Vague" and "not nailing it down" would lead one to believe that the explanation of the name as originating with the 1967 Pink Floyd single "Apples and Oranges" is unreliable, but it's always nice to be able to mention Pink Floyd, and I am happy to not be writing about the Oranges in Stereo.

"I came up with the name 'the Apples' while driving

around the countryside outside of Athens with Will Hart in the summer of 1992," Robert recalls. "It was the same car ride that Will came up with the name Elephant 6."

No matter how your local mom-and-pop record store or global streaming service might variously designate it, the Apples in Stereo was (or is) a Denver-based psychedelic pop (or "rock" if search engines are your thing) band that emerged from the seductive shadows and subsequent success of an ever-expanding musical community they co-created and carried. That same success obscured the Apples from the full recognition their music deserves.

Elephant 6, also known as the Elephant 6 Collective, or the Elephant 6 Recording Co., has been covered in the music media since the mid-nineties, often as a priority over the bands that comprised it. While the self-supporting nature of the collective was initially a rocket to underground notoriety, it unfortunately also shined the spotlight on the scene first and the scene makers second.

In the press, Robert was referred to as its driving motivation, in contrast with his ambivalence about being perceived that way by his friends and collaborators. A theatrically released documentary, *The Elephant 6 Recording Co.*, in 2022 valiantly attempted to consolidate its exceedingly complex story and may have included mentions of as many as ninety bands in ninety minutes.

More than thirty years earlier, "we decided to start our band after seeing the Fluid," Robert says about the Denver-based garage punk group. The Fluid was an important influence on the early nineties grunge scene after becoming the first non–Pacific Northwest signing to Sub Pop Records and releasing a split single with Nirvana in 1991.

Robert recalls, "They were doing a homecoming show. I

went with Hilarie, Jim, and Chris. When we left, we realized we *could* and, in fact, *had* to have a band."

Following his car ride outside Athens with Will Hart, the band Robert "had to have" began recording their debut EP in late 1992. The *Tidal Wave* EP—initially a cassette-only release—arrived in the spring of 1993. Robert estimates it was a lean nine months between the inspirational Fluid show and the practice space performance by the Apples celebrating *Tidal Wave*. The first cassette was sold that spring evening and the vinyl version of *Tidal Wave* became available soon after, in the summer of 1993.

I moved to Denver from Manhattan in 1995, and while I never saw the Fluid, I did see the beginnings of the rise of Elephant 6. The Apples signed a record deal with NYC-based indie label SpinART Records, which released the debut album *Fun Trick Noisemaker* that spring. The core lineup of the Jet, Fuzz, PRE, and Hilarie (nickname unknown) solidified soon after.

I first connected with Robert through my music industry beginnings, which eventually evolved into a decades-long career working with many artists I admire and helped to become admired.

At its start, my promotion company Fanatic focused on college radio. That is how I became familiar with the Apples. Unlike the vibrant cover art by Steve Keene for *Fun Trick Noisemaker*, which slipped past me, it was the jacket for *Science Faire*, the 1996 compilation of Apples material released prior to *Fun Trick Noisemaker* (including the *Tidal Wave* EP; its follow-up, the *Hypnotic Suggestion* EP from 1994; as well as other singles and B-sides) that got my attention.

In contrast to the *Fun Trick Noisemaker* cover, the black-

and-white image on the jacket of *Science Faire* appealed to me because of its dorky depiction of what looked like a seventies-era college radio station studio complete with bespectacled students at the controls. The Renaissance spelling of "Faire," and the band-naming conceit of "Projects by THE APPLES in stereo" served up an immediate invocation of lore.

I wanted to know more, and the actual lore is not a bore!

"The photo is of the original KLPI, Ruston radio station staff from the early seventies," Robert confirms enthusiastically. "It was a discarded extra photo that the station gave me when I was a teenager."

As it turns out, I was living 2.3 miles away from Robert and Hilarie at that time. It was 1996 and I hadn't met them yet, but I could already tell that they were artists who were only going to be understood by certain kinds of people.

Prior to digital distribution becoming standard, I was already impressed with what the Apples and Elephant 6 accomplished on their own, prior to signing to SpinART.

In the early nineties, during the infancy of the internet, it was much more difficult to record, release, and retail music in any kind of meaningful way without an established label, and much less so as a label without an organization that existed beyond its bands. I knew that Robert and Hilarie were doing it for the love of doing it. That purity is noticeable and appeals to people who relate to that attitude and way of life.

People who appreciate and become fans of artists who work passionately without pay know that they are being trusted with this sharing. It is a special kind of relationship that has scaled up throughout the decades as we see artists selling in the tens of millions while still maintaining that feeling of sharing and trust with their fans.

In 1996, college radio and zine culture were the ways that artists like the Apples in Stereo could connect directly with that era's version of a tastemaker, the kind of person who could hold a record like *Science Faire* in their hands and say, "These are my people."

My company grew, and although I moved thirty minutes away for more space in Boulder, I connected with Robert and Hilarie, and kept my eye on the development of Elephant 6, which I observed as a collective in name but rarely in reality.

"When you hear stories about potlucks in Athens, and they're describing sitting around, listening to somebody's record, at that exact moment halfway across the country, I was recording the *next* record," Robert says.

In Colorado, it was difficult to experience the Athens-based collective as anything other than esoteric, but soon "the Principal" would summon Neutral Milk Hotel to town to make *In the Aeroplane Over the Sea*.

"Maybe the world won't understand it, but at least other musicians will understand it," Robert said in a 2024 interview with the *Discograffiti* podcast about the origins of Elephant 6. Sometimes, however, even other musicians misunderstood Elephant 6, or found it perplexing or even irritating.

"Robert Pollard told me how we were perceived by the older lo-fi community," Robert says, recalling a conversation with the leader of the Dayton, Ohio–based lo-fi legends, Guided by Voices. Older lo-fi musicians were very kind and supportive of the Apples, but Robert S. says Robert P. told him that those same older lo-fi musicians resented Elephant 6.

"We stole their scene," Robert says.

"Robert and I were more about the label," Hilarie tells author Adam Clair in his book *Endless Endless: A*

Lo-Fi History of the Elephant 6 Mystery, highlighting a significant difference between the Denver- and Athens-based contingents of Elephant 6. "They were more about the collective."

"It was a practical organization effort," Robert says about why he designated the Athens group as "Elephant 6 East" and the Denver group as "Elephant 6 West."

As a fellow transplanted Coloradan, my personal connection to what looked like the development of a relatively minor but increasingly influential musical culture movement didn't feel like a connection to what looked like the development of a relatively minor but increasingly influential musical culture movement. It felt personal, like the kind of sharing and trust mentioned above. It felt like the philosophy and ideology that Robert says he wants all his collaborative connections, and his connections with fans, to be about: friendship.

As a personal ideal, this is what we all strive for. As a business, it can be a nonstarter at best and catastrophic at worst. For me, my friendship with Robert led to us getting together to work on some of my own songs at Pet Sounds.

I suppose Robert appeared slight to me at the time because everyone did—in the nineties, I was twice the size I am now—but the guy really did expend calories for two. His enthusiasm was like an additional presence in the room. We connected over songwriting, our similar sense of humor, and *The Simpsons*.

"I used to shut the studio down from five to seven to watch *Simpsons* reruns," he reminds me. Robert told me recently that the tapes containing the songs we worked on together are now with the Elephant 6 archives at the University of Georgia.

With the perspective of thirty years, it is clear how the Apples in Stereo exist apart from the Elephant 6 scene, or any "scene," frankly. At the time, however, it was not possible to fully understand the eventual artistic impact that the band's representation of the reemerging sound of mid-to-late sixties psychedelic pop post-*Nevermind* would have.

Fun Trick Noisemaker was released less than three years removed from the formation of the Apples, and four years after the culture-shifting impact of *Nevermind*. Their debut album captures that same spirit of abandoning conventional norms of commercial pop in favor of the raw and genuine sonic approach that remains ridiculously melodious and catchy nonetheless.

"I remember seeing the 'Smells Like Teen Spirit' video on MTV when it debuted," Robert says. "I was really impressed. Hilarie saw the band play in Boulder, but I had not heard them yet, and was like, 'Wow! They look just like me and my friends instead of like posers.'"

Of course, by that time, guided by the tacit direction of Kurt Cobain, Nirvana was already a music industry commodity. However, even in death, or perhaps because of it, Kurt remains an archetype for uncompromising artistic integrity combined with uncompromising commercial ambition. You don't become the biggest band in the world without participating in your ascension.

"It's a model of pretending to take things seriously—the Elephant 6 logo isn't even trademarked!" author Adam Clair writes in *Endless Endless*.

If the organization of Elephant 6 as a business had been taken more seriously, or had even been more serious about becoming organized in the first place, the Apples may very well continue to exist as a productive and profitable legacy indie rock act with the trajectory and respect of Yo La Tengo (which—like the Apples did at the time—contains a husband and wife), or They Might Be Giants (which contains two hetero life mates), or Pavement (which contains Stephen Malkmus), just to name a few.

Today, bands like these "play the game" to some degree—no "indie" band gets to play at Nirvana levels anymore—while remaining artistically independent as a given. Because of this, these artists are more self-sustaining than ever and are revered by more fans than ever *because* of sticking to these ideals over the decades. The Apples didn't survive into the era when artists on their own labels could take advantage of everything the music industry offers in terms of organization and opportunity.

Robert recounts a story later of walking into his record label's office and throwing all the band's glossy photos (remember those?) in the trash because the image had not been approved. No record label would print unapproved materials today. It would be not only considered disrespectful to the artist and their fans but an embarrassment to the art.

We are now in an era where integrity is a commodity in and of itself, and with that, the one immovable requirement is more important than ever: great songs. The Apples have lots of 'em.

My ten-second elevator pitch for Robert might not even mention the Apples in Stereo first.

Q: "Who is Robert Schneider?"

A: "He produced one of *Rolling Stone*'s '500 Greatest Albums of All Time.'"

My discussions with Robert tell me that this milestone

feels like a pebble in his shoe sometimes. I will share as much as I can about why.

Depending on if Robert's mom was in that elevator, I would swap out my answer with "His biggest song was performed by the Top 5 contestants on *American Idol* as part of the show's weekly advertorial segment for Ford."

By the way, this is the first time I have ever typed the word "advertorial" in my entire life.

That said, Robert's legacy primarily exists for music fans as a part of the sum of the band, the collective, and all the triumph and trauma created at the intersection of the two. It is unique for a rock group to be so closely associated with a scene that the association becomes like an albatross at times.

It's as if the Beatles had come out of, but remained closely associated with, the "Cavern Club Collective," and felt obligated to spend valuable time both nurturing and relying on it like some kind of caustic crutch. In a way, the Beatles did retroactively try something like this with the formation of the money-burning operation Apple Corps.

That particular focus-fracturing entrepreneurial endeavor ended with the short-lived Apple clothing boutique—one of the many Apple Corps businesses that came and went—giving away all its merchandise on the day it went out of business. As a songwriting entity, the Beatles sadly went out of business shortly thereafter too.

After some prodding, Robert lays it out.

"I was a member of a band, and we were a team, and I was the team leader. But I also was a supporter. On top of that, I was the producer, and that was a different thing, and I also did that for other bands. On top of that, I was the collective leader, and that was a different thing, and I did that for even more bands than I produced. I don't think I had a model for any other human being that did that. It was a lot! I had to figure it out all on my own, and looking back, it feels like I lived the life of ten people."

If you feel a sense of anxiety from reading Robert's recollection, you are not alone!

But there's more!

"The Apples were the sandbox in which I worked out my philosophies and my engineering skills so that I could further the ambitions of everyone around me, as well as my own. Everyone is obsessed with what was going on in Athens, including me, but the Apples were before that and made it possible."

Even with Robert donning so many hats, it's not as if he came up short wearing any of them. It is that he had to develop a style that included wearing them all at the same time, and I don't think we have ever seen somebody look their best trying to rock a swagger while balancing multiple hats on their head.

"I'm saying all this, not because I'm personally concerned about me," he confides. "I am concerned about our band, our music, our stories, and my bandmates getting recognition."

By the time the sixth Apples album *New Magnetic Wonder* was released in 2007, Robert was fifteen years into the band's existence, and even with the sudden change brought by Hilarie's departure from the group, the Apples in Stereo found their biggest success on that road to recognition.

"'Energy' is our flagship song," Robert says of *New Magnetic Wonder*'s first single.

As far as metrics, "Energy" is indeed the most popular song by the Apples with close to ten million plays on Spotify alone. The song was blown up by a Pepsi commercial, it is sometimes covered in concert by Phish, and, as previously mentioned, it was performed on the 2009 season of *American Idol*. The band's label boss at the time, celebrity actor Elijah Wood, made his directorial debut with the music video for the song, which is currently threatening to pass a million views on YouTube.

With this information, my preconceived bias about the *New Magnetic Wonder* album is being both confronted and confirmed by the knowledge of these corporate, big-business, and fame-adjacent associations, but I come up with criticisms of Spotify, Pepsi, Phish, and *Idol* to dig myself back in. I'll give Elijah a break. He seemed to be having fun running a record label, and a year after releasing the Apples album *Travellers in Space and Time* in 2010, he portrayed Ad-Rock of the Beastie Boys in the music video for the song "Make Some Noise," alongside actors Seth Rogan as MCA and Danny McBride as Mike D. I can't front on that.

Even though Hilarie is the drummer on "Energy," when I mention that it was performed by *Idol* contestants, she is very surprised.

"It was?!" she exclaims.

Sixteen years later, Hilarie says she had no idea, and I claim that fact as another point of confirmation bias!

If there was ever a peek into what a moment of mainstream Apples post-graduation from Elephant 6 would look like, "Energy" was it. But even with the band's rejuvenated lineup, and consistently solid reviews for the album—a further affront to what I had already decided about *New Magnetic Wonder*—I sense that Robert was still wrestling with what the next level of notoriety would mean.

"People who are rich, famous, or whatever . . . they are owned by society," Robert says. "They are owned by the public. Fame is not a property of a person like talent is.

Fame, and similarly, money, is a property of the public."

Fame is not as interesting as notoriety. Fame is a man-made and created idea derived from the external forces that we place on a person. What's weird about that is this elevation has little to do with what is actually being elevated.

Fame gained through producing pretty photographs of your above-average visage is the result of the mere mass cultural awareness of its existence. Notoriety, on the other hand, means that people are talking about something they can't see.

> It's like the bird
> That you can't see
> But you can hear the pretty music in the tree
> —"The Bird That You Can't See" from *The Discovery of a World Inside the Moone*

More pointedly and personally, in Adam Clair's *Endless Endless*, Robert states, "I hate money. Money ruined Elephant 6. Money's bad. There's nothing good about it. The only thing good about it is having it when you don't. It's just one of the dimensions of human life. We have space, we have time, and we have money. Money is more like time. Time doesn't end well. Money's that way, too."

To that end, when I bring up the idea that many talented young songwriters would love to hire the mind and skills behind the production of an album they revere, which also happens to be one of *Rolling Stone*'s "500 Greatest Albums of All Time," namely *In the Aeroplane Over the Sea* by Neutral Milk Hotel, Robert makes it clear that leaving money on the table is exactly where he would like to leave it.

How does this point of view square with the use of

"Energy" in a Pepsi commercial? I ask Robert this question later, but at the moment, during a discussion of how money corrupts, and specifically how it can corrupt professional relationships, friendships, and marriages, I point out that the Elephant 6 documentary film makes no mention of Hilarie leaving the band after fourteen years. It simply cuts to a shot where she has now been replaced by drummer John Dufilho (of the Deathray Davies) miming to her performance in the video for "Energy," the flagship song that generated more money in licensing fees than album sales.

I am fair and fairly candid! I think voicing this observation hits a nerve.

Robert replies dismissively, "Yes—I guess all the bands had comings and goings in the big picture. Remember, I am a storyteller who builds myths around my friends and colleagues, and that is the last I will say about that."

I sense Robert is hurt or annoyed, neither of which was my intent. We are all in a constant state of reinvention. This is a phenomenon pertaining to all people, but when it comes to artists who happen to be former (or current?) members of a band, they are prone to publicly rewriting their professional histories for personal reasons when they go solo, or the band breaks up.

What if we heard Paul McCartney say, "John Lennon. Good guy! We were in a band together fifty years ago! Let's talk about Wings!"

Morrissey has actually offered an actual take similar to this in recent years in regard to his songwriting partnership with Johnny Marr in the Smiths.

Of course, fans find this assertion ridiculous because we are so connected to the emotions the songs evoke in us that we can't imagine such a dismissive statement being anything other than a mask covering trauma and pain.

Revisionist history is everyone's default, and is not necessarily intentional. I am telling this story as a person who has little interest, motivation, or ability to revise that history, but the passing of decades should be taken into account when reading about the Apples in Stereo.

Whether the subjects remember, relate, or are even enlightened by my commentary is irrelevant. If it brings you closer to the music fixed in perpetuity, that is all that matters. Notwithstanding deluxe, remixed, and remastered reissues, the stories in the songs can never be revised.

Apple Picking, Pt. One
"Tidal Wave" from *Fun Trick Noisemaker*

Throughout this book, you can take pit stops ("seed stops"? I'm sorry, but I warned you that the apple puns were coming!) to read about some specific songs. I asked Robert, Hilarie, John, and Eric to name—without cheating!—a few tunes that immediately popped into their minds. As some of these songs enter the narrative, we will explore them. It makes perfect sense to start at the start. Robert, Eric, and John all mentioned "Tidal Wave" when I posed the question.

"'Tidal Wave' defined the early Apples," John says.

The credited songwriters of "Tidal Wave" are Robert Schneider and Chris Parfitt, whom I mentioned previously as part of the gang at that precipitous Denver show by the Fluid. Chris was a member of the Apples during the brief time when they were *only* the Apples, without the "in stereo," but his part in their history is secured by this key song in the band's catalog.

"Tidal Wave" is a uniquely special song by the Apples in

Stereo, especially for the fact that it essentially bookends the band's entire career. The song is the first track on the first Apples EP, and that EP is the first release by any Elephant 6 band. It is the first to display the iconic Will Hart–created Elephant 6 logo, which still appears today on new record releases, concert posters, and quality hoodies available online now in all your favorite fall fashion colors!

(L–R): Robert Schneider, Hilarie Sidney, Joel Morowitz (the late cofounder of SpinART Records), and John Hill seen during the shooting of the "Tidal Wave" music video. "Joel stood in on bass for the video," Robert explains of the period just before Eric Allen joined the group. "He was such a sweet man who believed in us so hard." Courtesy of the Apples in Stereo.

"We wrote it together, even before we started to play with Jim and Hilarie," Robert says. "'Tidal Wave' wasn't just the first Apples song anyone heard; it was the first Apples song we ever wrote! Chris and I were sitting together, jamming. The moment of creation happened between us, it was shared, and it felt like a revelation as we started to play the riff together in my apartment."

The version of "Tidal Wave" that appears on the band's 1993 debut EP was later rerecorded for the 1995 debut album *Fun Trick Noisemaker* after John Hill joined the band, replacing Chris.

In the opening seven seconds of the new version, the band's mandate is established. Cut to thirty years later and those same seconds are what we hear when the trailer of *The Elephant 6 Recording Co.* documentary opens. Just like the first few seconds of a single are meant to hook you into the album, the first few seconds of a movie trailer are meant to hook you into the movie.

The first thing we hear is Hilarie's calamitous drums followed by that memorable "moment of creation" riff.

"Yes! Hilarie's drums, and then it is both me and John Hill coming in, doubling the main riff," Robert explains. "There is also a Moog MG-1 synthesizer playing the same riff as well, so it sounds like a tight ball of fuzz. It gives awesome riffage. Doubled rhythm guitars with fuzz synthesizer. It sounds really tight, and you don't hear the synth. I use the same method on 'I Can't Believe' (from 2000's *The Discovery of a World Inside the Moone*). That's my secret trick!"

Secret revealed!

"I didn't think about it until you said it, but that's really nice," Robert responds when I point out how "Tidal Wave" introduced the Apples to the world and the song also opens the trailer of the documentary *about* introducing the Apples to the world. "It is the window into the early era of the Apples, a post-grunge psych band practicing in the bowels of a condemned yogurt factory in Denver," Robert says. "It's our original spark!"

Robert clarifies that we hear Jim McIntyre playing

bass on both the EP and album versions of the song. Eric Allen joined the Apples in Stereo on bass in 1995 after the recording of *Fun Trick Noisemaker*.

The instantly recognizable opening riff by Kurt Cobain on "Smells Like Teen Spirit" is the first noise that most of the world heard from Nirvana (the cool kids heard *Bleach*), but it's the blown-down doors of Dave Grohl's entrance on the track that throttles us.

The unassailable three seconds of John Lennon's "Shoot me!" followed by the instantly recognizable lefty playing right of Ringo's across-the-kit drum fill on "Come Together" by the Beatles is already playing in your head as you complete this sentence. Changing music history in under three seconds is not hyperbole!

Jack White has said that Meg White was the best part of the White Stripes. Preceding that duo's debut album by four years, the opening seconds of the *Fun Trick Noisemaker* version of "Tidal Wave" represent Hilarie's percussion purpose in the same less-is-more way that later became Meg's musical mission statement.

Karen Carpenter and Moe Tucker carved out a place of respect and awe for women drummers in the late sixties. Now it is Hilarie's turn.

When I first met Hilarie, I was struck by how her sweet, smart personality matched her voice and lyrics, and her toughness matched her drumming. It was clear that the warm woman carving me a serving of Tofurky on Thanksgiving could quickly cock her head to shake aside her long blond hair, and I would instantly be reminded of the knife she was holding there.

Put down this book and listen to the first seven seconds of "Tidal Wave" again.

THE APPLES IN STEREO

Are you back? What sounds like the chaos of drums and cymbals being intentionally thrown down a set of steep concrete steps is the relentless trap attack of Hilarie Sidney.

3. THE APPLE IN MONO: "I AM FILLED WITH FIRE"

We expect artists to express themselves authentically in their songs. Otherwise, why are they worth listening to? They certainly wouldn't be worth writing about. If you are interested in what Robert tells us about himself as a songwriter, recording artist, and producer, then please let what you learn here bring you back to the Apples in Stereo with that perspective. Feel free to take a headphone break!

Public and media perspectives on Robert Schneider as a songwriter, recording artist, and producer have been set for years, and there isn't much to say about the technicalities, ins and outs, and day-to-day aspects of being a songwriter, recording artist, and producer that are substantially different from one to another. This book is likely not the first band bio you've read, so you likely already understand this.

What is unique, worth discussing, and documenting is the person behind those titles. Who can speak more substantially about who Robert is, or more specifically, who is willing to speak more substantially about who Robert is? We can learn so much more about people when we listen to what they tell us about *themselves*, through what they choose not to tell us.

●

"Today marks the forty-seventh anniversary of my family's move to the US from South Africa," Robert wrote in a public Facebook post in September 2024. "After a slow start in childhood, I made a lot of friends—but I live my life as an outsider, known by few, a wanderer without a home.

"I saw the Statue of Liberty from the window of our airplane as we landed in New York, it stands out in my memory as the symbol of my new home. We all huddle and wish for acceptance.

"The Statue of Liberty says each of us can find our place in American society. I believe in that promise even though it is not yet achieved."

As anyone who has ever interviewed Robert throughout the decades will attest, he sticks with the conversation until he loses interest, which is exactly never. Every interview with Robert is an in-depth interview.

He has been tagged with the backhanded compliment "mad genius" before, a lazy summation that negates the subject and simplifies the work. We are all objectively mad geniuses. In Robert's case, this stereotype starts with the way he communicates.

The words come so quickly, from so many different directions, and encompassing so many different thoughts that some journalists seem to excuse their waving of the white flag by deciding that Robert is just too quirky to comprehend.

This is convenient considering he is an artist, and therefore is already relegated to being thought of as "weird," because aren't all artists "weird"?

"I was kicked out of three kindergartens and sent back

to preschool with the evaluation that I could not be taught," he tells me.

Robert's institutional difficulties continued through failing high school algebra, but he eventually proved these lifelong learning evaluations wildly incorrect. Robert was forced to give math another go when he needed to maintain the Ampex MM-1200 two-inch sixteen-track tape machine he acquired in 1998 for his studio, Pet Sounds.

Unfolded schematics on the studio floor led to the unfolding of a new life. Robert now holds a PhD in mathematics from Emory University in Atlanta.

During his doctoral work in 2018, Robert was interviewed for a piece about him by *Atlanta* magazine, in which his doctoral adviser, Ken Ono, commented, "He's very difficult to advise because he's confident, he's creative, and it's very important to him that the work he does is completely of his creation.

"On one hand, that means his work is going to be beautiful, but it makes it more difficult for me to show how his work is connected to the work of others."

This observation by a mathematician about Robert's relationship with mathematics and the work of other mathematicians is fascinating because of its unintentional connection to Robert's music career.

I am not comparing myself to a doctoral adviser in mathematics, but when I began writing about Robert's artistic life, I also found it difficult to show exactly how Robert's work is connected to the work of others. I am sure that Ken figured out how to do that, and I will too.

The trick to understanding Robert is to adjust your perceptions about where the point he is making is going while simultaneously preparing yourself to tie together the different strands of thought to make them whole within your own mind.

Sometimes, you don't know if Robert is giving you what he thinks you want, if he is giving you what he thinks will maintain his mystery, or if he is giving you just enough demystification to cause you to conclude your line of questioning prematurely.

Robert is a mathematician, after all, and so he is always solving a social equation. You may find what he communicates crystal clear, or, in piecing together his stream of consciousness, you may find your version of the truth. I believe Robert when he says he has lived his life as "an outsider, known by few."

If you listen closely to Robert's songs and his productions, most notably his collaborations with Jeff Mangum of Neutral Milk Hotel, you can become one of those few.

The former—the songs—seem like the obvious way in. The latter—the production—requires more explanation. The word "collaboration" is intentional. Robert provides more information than you will ever need. Processing all of it is the challenge.

Robert has arrived at some hard truths over the thirty years I have known him. These include truths that he has arrived at through personal growth, truths he trusted me enough to confide in, and truths he felt he had to follow up to say must stay off the record.

Fair and fairly candid. We did spend studio break time watching *The Simpsons* together after all.

Record producer Ken Callait had to sue the Broadway show *Stereophonic*, claiming that the play, which centers around a band making an album, copied elements from his memoir *Making Rumours*.

The lawsuit was later settled.

This may be the first time you have heard of Ken. His role in the making of *Rumours*—one of the most celebrated albums in history—has never been at the forefront of discussions about Fleetwood Mac. It is likely that music journalists, even if they are Fleetwood Mac fans themselves, had never heard of Ken before writing about this lawsuit.

Unlike Ken's working relationship with Fleetwood Mac, Robert's relationship with Jeff Mangum of Neutral Milk Hotel dates back to when they were just boys in the single digits.

(L–R): Hilarie Sidney, Robert Schneider, and Jeff Mangum in the early nineties during the days before making one of Rolling Stone's *"500 Greatest Albums of All Time." "It was our first tour out West," Robert remembers of the period prior to producing Jeff's debut record. "The Apples and Neutral Milk Hotel were basically one band in a minivan." Photo by Lisa Janssen, courtesy of the Apples in Stereo.*

To people like me who grew up reading *Rolling Stone*, it is incredibly impressive that *In the Aeroplane Over the Sea* by Neutral Milk Hotel, a beloved album that Robert produced, was named one of *Rolling Stone*'s "500 Greatest Albums of All Time."

This career bullet point can be dropped anywhere, and it will mean something significant to anyone who is remotely a fan of popular music. *Rolling Stone* is known to every person connected to rock music just like *Saturday Night Live* is known to every person connected to comedy or just like the Academy Awards are known to every person connected to film.

For the producers of *Stereophonic*, Ken Callait had to have his role in *Rumours*, via his memoir, clarified in arbitration fifty years after the fact. The role of a record producer can take on different forms, depending on the producer and the artist.

"I also have to give Robert credit for writing most of the horn parts," Neutral Milk Hotel's Scott Spillane explains in Adam Clair's *Endless Endless*, talking about the parts Robert composed for Scott to perform on *In the Aeroplane Over the Sea*.

Regarding those parts, Eric Allen adds, "So many Neutral Milk Hotel melodies that people sing in their heads were written by Robert. I find myself humming the trombone lines more than the vocals. I'm not taking anything away from Jeff, but Robert's contribution has been underappreciated."

"PRE is really kind," Robert replies, sticking strictly to Eric's given nickname. "Jeff's vocal melodies are iconic and super catchy, but I think it's true that the horn parts are also catchy?"

Robert's humility annoys me sometimes!

It is extraordinary to see footage of thousands of Neutral Milk Hotel fans singing Robert's horn melodies back to the stage.

Referring to songs on the Neutral Milk Hotel albums *On Avery Island* and *In the Aeroplane Over the Sea*, Robert recalls, "I developed almost all of the melodies that were not vocal melodies.

"The organ in 'Naomi' and the horns on 'Holland' and 'Song Against Sex' are major hooks too, I guess, like the air organ line in 'Carrot Flowers.'"

Robert also developed innovative production techniques to accomplish a signature distortion sound throughout the album.

"You should know that I don't like my own voice," he says. "I would rather hear other singers. That album expressed my ideas through Jeff's songs. Our goal was to make a classic. So it was on purpose."

It is good to hear this. Robert doesn't publicly take enough credit for what he has brought into the world, and in public is where it counts. Is this a remnant of the "no selling out" post-*Nevermind* disease, as stated earlier?

Maybe he is tempering egomania? Maybe he just forgot to take credit, like after the Apples signed with SpinART and Robert would accidentally wash off interview appointments that he had written reminders for on his wrist.

"I do not receive royalties on Neutral Milk Hotel for being a producer, performer, or arranger," Robert says.

This, despite Jeff saying to *Exclaim!* magazine in 1998, as referenced in Adam Clair's *Endless Endless*, "I think of *On Avery Island* as more of a collaborative effort between me and Robert."

Being in the business, I figured Robert being cut out was the case, but it still makes me angry on his behalf. I get the impression there are lingering feelings that have nothing to do with money and everything to do with honor and respect.

When we are younger and rebelling, we are in business even when we think we are not in business because we believe we are rejecting the kind of business agreements that make business "business." This attitude that we are not aware of at the time creates unresolved lifelong conflicts. Handshake agreements become headshake disagreements.

Because Pet Sounds existed as the studio destination for the core Elephant 6 bands, Robert's relationship as the producer on paper (there was no paper!) was often collaborative to a point far beyond the role a producer would typically play.

This would most definitely be the case with an artist Robert was friends with since the time that they were both boys in the single digits.

"Robert was as much a band member as the producer," author Kim Cooper writes in her 2005 book about *In the Aeroplane Over the Sea*.

I wonder if the reason we never got another Neutral Milk Hotel record is because only Robert could ever be able to understand Jeff's sensitivities and harness his eccentricities. No collaborator besides Robert could ever be able to know Jeff so well.

My anger turns to sadness, but only for a moment.

I remember that there is literally a single comment from Jeff in *The Elephant 6 Recording Co.* documentary in which he says the records wouldn't be as special without Robert. That's all we hear about that. I will give Jeff the benefit of the doubt that he said more that was left on the cutting-room floor.

Robert can ignite when he feels like his art is being compromised by the will of others, even if those others are his teammates, bandmates, or collaborators, but when it comes to the business of art, which is underlined by Robert's stated hatred of money, he seems to need forcing to be less humble on purpose, unlike how he naturally made a classic on purpose.

This is not criticism. This is advocacy! Too many artists are cheated, marginalized, or forgotten because they don't demand what is theirs. Everyone has their reasons, boundaries, and hang-ups. But propriety, respect, and plain old "doing what's right" is what young Robert saw when he was greeted by the Statue of Liberty those forty-seven years ago.

All artists should be aware of danger when signing off on a master recording that represents the artist, the work, and, most importantly, what will ultimately be the enduring story of the artist and the work.

Now that you see Robert as a sympathetic figure, let's mess with that!

"You can quote me on anything, unless I'm being a dick," Robert jokes. (I think?)

Since I'm not sure, I reply, "Can I quote you on that?"

Robert shoots back, "Just kidding! I'm always a dick!"

I love that Robert is not above calling himself out as a full-time dick. It feels like maybe he does it himself so he doesn't have to bear having it done to him. Unlike most people, the more you push Robert, the more he will give. But that generosity comes with a warning: You may not like what you get.

"If Robert ever gets pissed off, there's a whole other side to him," Jeff Price, the cofounder of SpinART Records, says in *Endless Endless*.

Robert details one incident from the "other side," saying, "We contractually had creative control, and we approved a certain publicity photo, and when we got to their office, it turned out that SpinART had selected what they thought was a better photo and printed up a whole stack of glossies.

"I took the entire stack, completely tore it up, and threw it in the trash. A total waste of money. But I had to claim our creative control. I acted like an ass, but it was righteous anger to protect us," Robert explains. "Our whole scene viewed the music industry as kind of poaching on us. Full creative control was a very touchy issue that I valued more than money or exposure, and I flew off the handle."

I checked with Robert again to make sure he was okay with being perceived as a dick before telling the "Glossies in the Garbage" story. He responded with a deep truth. The kind of truth I am talking about when it comes to artists expressing themselves authentically in their songs. I hope it stays with you subconsciously the next time you listen to the Apples in Stereo.

"I want to be seen as a fire," Robert shares. "That's what it feels like to be me on the inside. On the outside, you usually feel a warm glow, but sometimes there are flames. They are flames of emotion and words, not actions!"

Robert describes himself next in a way I relate to so much. I would never have thought to describe my own pacifist personality this way, but I will in the future. Maybe you will too.

"I would never give blows," he says. "But I might be

willing to say things that would cause me to receive blows."

"I want to be seen as a fire, not a glow," Robert repeats. "This is something about myself that other people don't understand. You seem to understand it," he tells me, "and Jeff Price got it, somewhat unusually.

"This was not my only big rage moment, but they are few and far between, usually in righteous anger, and always regrettable," he admits. "There is a better way to handle things, but I just hadn't worked it out yet then, and I still haven't. The flames are very hot and I regret them. I wish I had a copy of that lost photo now to remember."

This last statement makes me think more about Robert's ongoing personal growth. How he has come to terms with injustice, and how he feels about his work as a songwriter, recording artist, and producer as he is discovered by new fans, in this new light—fans who weren't even alive when he was that earlier version of himself.

I am shocked all over again contemplating the tragedy of Robert's best friends not being allowed that same chance. Bill and Will because they are gone from the planet, and Jeff because he is gone from public life and music-making.

"There's a long piece at the end of *On Avery Island*, the very, very long piece with the drone that ends with the gamelan piece," Robert told author Kim Cooper twenty years ago. "It's probably one of the favorite things that I've ever worked on."

Just shy of three decades later, Robert tells me, "That drone is the pinnacle of my production career. It's the studio story I retell—well, my living room studio."

He adds, "It is my big engineering moment, like the cymbal crash for Hilarie."

*"Drive down to Denver," he said. "We'll work on some of your songs,"
he said. When Robert invited me over to Pet Sounds, I didn't expect
to see a building that looked like this! Yet, somehow, so much musical
magic was made at 1170 Elati Street. Photo by Robert Schneider,
courtesy of the Apples in Stereo.*

4. PET SOUNDS, PTS. ONE & TWO

Robert wanted to take our recording budgets and buy equipment with them so we could create our own sonic worlds.

—Eric Allen

Pt. One: "It's Part of the Writing of Songs for Us"

Hearts and promises were broken in this room.

I remember the dank entryway of Pet Sounds, Robert's recording studio that existed on the ground floor of a building battered beyond belief. It felt like encountering the concrete emptiness on the other side of a just-lowered manual garage door during a wet Colorado snowstorm with the sound of the metal guide rails scraping their way into the soft flesh of your brain forever.

It is a good thing for music obsessives that 1170 Elati Street in Denver wasn't torn down before 1999. I hope that the residents of the luxury condos that were subsequently built there know that they live where fabled music was made. Maybe there are a few hipsters upstairs who own copies of Robert's productions without even knowing that they were created just beneath their feet.

The murals that artist Steve Keene created for the Pet

Sounds control room walls can be seen in the music video for "Tidal Wave."

Murals by Steve Keene in the Pet Sounds control room. Steve also painted the cover of the debut Apples album Fun Trick Noisemaker, *and is one of the world's most prolific artists, having sold or given away more than three hundred thousand paintings. Photo by Robert Schneider, courtesy of the Apples in Stereo.*

Hilarie's red Rogers Holiday drum set is here; the "house kit," as I suggest to Robert. "Yes! House kit! Just like at Motown. That was my goal because I knew how to get good sound!"

I later ask Hilarie if she still owns the set. "Yes, I do! Fun fact: Kurt Heasley (of the Lilys) bought it for me."

According to Robert, the Rogers set also appears on the

Elephant 6 classics *Music from the Unrealized Film Script: Dusk at Cubist Castle* and *Black Foliage: Animation Music Volume One*, both by the Olivia Tremor Control, as well as the Neutral Milk Hotel masterpiece *In the Aeroplane Over the Sea.*

Aeroplane is the most well-known and popular record to come out of this room. Type "In the Ae" in the YouTube search bar and it comes up as the top result. Speaking of iconic drums, just "In the A" returns "In the Air Tonight" by Phil Collins.

Robert pictured at the console of the Pet Sounds control room in Denver during the studio's heyday. This is where the most revered Elephant 6 releases were made. Robert is wearing what he calls his "fancy shirt." Photo by Hilarie Sidney, courtesy of the Apples in Stereo.

Just behind the classic album by the Beach Boys that named it, Pet Sounds Recording Studio is music history's second most important Pet Sounds. In the late nineties, a decade or more before comfortable, well-equipped, and computer-driven home studios could be built with a meager budget, Robert's room wasn't only without glamour, it was damn near with squalor.

It doesn't matter. So many records we adore wouldn't hit as hard if not for the environment in which they were made. In 1996, this room had everything Robert needed to change the world.

"We hated the sound of stuff that came out of commercial studios," Robert said to *Tape Op* ("A magazine about creative music recording") as a seasoned record producer, for issue no. 155 of the publication in 2018. "The idea of going into a place and having them make you sound different from the way you felt you sounded."

Twenty-two years earlier, the not-so-seasoned record producer was previously interviewed for issue no. 2 of the magazine. "We're always gonna do our records on our own. We'll just get higher budgets and more great equipment. Someday we'll have a 16-track, maybe," Robert said in 1996.

"In the first *Tape Op* interview, I had just acquired our equipment and had not yet finished our first album," Robert remembers. "I was really impressed with all of our cheap gear at the time! I love reading the two interviews together because they bookend the years as one statement."

This proof of Robert's consistent record-making philosophy over such a long stretch of time is another point that goes toward his argument with me about why I should appreciate *New Magnetic Wonder* and *Travellers in Space and Time* more.

I bat that notion away for now, thinking, *If my mind is going to be changed, it is the songs that will do the persuading*, but later I persuade Robert to persuade me.

As it turns out, the 1996 interview was considered important. As stated previously, recording and releasing your own records in the late nineties was not as easy as it is today. "Other kids told me that they read it and then made studios," Robert says. "If that's true, then it's probably my greatest interview ever!"

I felt bad for three days when I began to write about Pet Sounds. I wondered if I had misremembered that the studio smelled like cat pee, and when Hilarie did not answer me about it, I stopped asking questions and started feeling guilty.

Later, when I watched the *Elephant 6* documentary and saw interviews about stray cats being fed there, I felt like less of a jerk, especially when Eric Allen popped up in the film to say that they had nicknamed the place "Pet Smells," which, of course, a band with a strict nicknaming policy would do.

"It smelled sooooo bad!" Eric wrote back when I told him this story.

John Hill diplomatically leaves it at "I wasn't crazy about that studio or the dynamics there."

Robert is nonplussed (or is it "non-pussed" in the case of cats?).

"Have I told you about the cats on *On Avery Island*?" he responds in classic Robert fashion of taking whatever you ask, using it as a pivot point, and then asking a new question that is more interesting than the one you wanted an answer to.

"They all gathered around the speakers when I composed that drone at the end of the album! The upshot is, they like experimental music. This is further proof. For millions of years, cats have had no access to music. Now they have synthesizers!"

Robert is referring to the pair of felines we both watch online named Tony and Frankie whose owner gives them synthesizers to step on and then selectively cuts in and out of the footage at the just the right moments to transform these two cats into compositional geniuses who would never ever pee in a recording studio.

Again, it doesn't matter if cats of lesser elegance marked their territory at Pet Sounds. Art isn't about where you make the art. Art is about where the art makes you. To the lives lifted by Jeff Mangum's stirring "I love you, Jesus Kuh-riiiiiiiiiiist!" on "The King of Carrot Flowers, Pts. Two & Three," the permanence of Robert's contributions to the lifting of those lives may not be immediately known, but these impermanent walls know all.

In the Aeroplane Over the Sea is the rare record that stands within, above, and beyond the environment in which it was conceived and created, all at the same time.

Surprisingly, this landmark version of Pet Sounds was actually an upgrade. 1170 Elati had its own front door onto the street instead of a bedroom door into a friend's hallway.

In an era when major labels were beginning to fly lo-fi garage bands into million-dollar rooms in major cities, Robert was ecstatic just to fire up the VU meters on his very own reel-to-reel machine.

Robert (referring to the photo on the opposite page): "This is me as we began our first record, in the just-assembled temporary recording studio that we built at our friend Brandt Larson's parents' house in Glendora, California. We had just gotten powered up for the first time, and I am excited to begin our path forward! This was both the control room and the recording room for the sessions that began *Fun Trick Noisemaker.* We recorded most of the live and backing tracks here, and then the album was completed at Kyle Jones's house in Denver."

Robert adds, "I think the idea of Pet Sounds officially

Robert has been including Brian Wilson references in recording studio shots since the start. "My fire hat is a reference to Brian," he explains. Brian was known to wear one just like it during his most chaotic recording sessions. Photo by Hilarie Sidney, courtesy of the Apples in Stereo.

begins with this photo in California." Upon returning to Denver to continue work on *Fun Trick Noisemaker*, Kyle's house became the first studio that Robert actually named Pet Sounds.

After 1170 Elati was scheduled to be torn down, Pet Sounds reemerged for a short time at 1971 Roslyn Street in Denver.

Okay, at least Pet Sounds didn't look like this when I showed up to record with Robert! Here we see the last days of 1170 Elati Street just prior to its demolition in 1999. Condominiums stand in the space today. Photo by Robert Schneider, courtesy of the Apples in Stereo.

"I stopped producing other artists in 2000," Robert says. "Having a baby (Robert and Hilarie's son Max was born that year) changed my perspective and my priorities."

Robert, Hilarie, and Max eventually relocated to Lexington, Kentucky, in 2002 to be closer to Hilarie's parents.

"We literally sent the *Velocity of Sound* tapes (the band's 2002 album release) to (Brooklyn-based producer and engineer) Bryce Goggin to mix on our way out of town and arrived in Kentucky to start receiving his mixes to comment on," Robert recalls.

As for leaving 1170 Elati, hearts and promises were

broken in this room, and even though Robert and Hilarie left forever, there was still more heartbreaking to do. Pet Sounds remained located in Lexington through the release of the last Apples album *Travellers in Space and Time* in 2010, after which Robert moved with Marci (Schneider, Robert's wife), and Max to Atlanta to pursue his current career in mathematics. Hilarie permanently relocated to Grøa, Norway, in 2014.

While the door is no more, the music on the master tapes once stored behind it continues to find new fans every day. "Tape Storage," as seen through the smashed window of the just-about-to-be-torn-down building at 1170 Elati Street in Denver, where Pet Sounds Recording Studio once stood. Photo by Robert Schneider, courtesy of the Apples in Stereo.

Where are the pieces of Pet Sounds now?

As it goes with many studios, when the Pet Sounds gear was eventually disassembled, much of it was parsed out to new owners.

"I gave most of it away years ago," Robert says. "Some of

it went to the Elephant 6 archive at the University of Georgia, and some of it is at the studio Chase Park Transduction in Athens. Hilarie and the other Apples have a few pieces, preamps, and microphones."

"I took it to Kentucky, and we used it for some years there," Robert says of the Ampex MM-1200 two-inch sixteen-track tape machine. "It started to fall into disuse and then into disrepair, so I gave it to Bryce," the producer and engineer mentioned above whom the Apples began working with when he mixed *Velocity of Sound*.

"Bryce drove out with a van to pick it up. It had become a burden, but also deserved to be used. Michelangelo's *David* would become a burden if you had to move it all the time!"

But, but, but . . . what about the Otari MX-5050 tape machine that all the most treasured Elephant 6 songs were recorded on (as well as the unfinished, and therefore unfortunately not-treasured, Josh Bloom songs)?

"I really regret not finishing those," Robert says of my tunes. "We were very close and the productions were amazing and the songs were amazing." Of course, I quote Robert praising my songs, because why wouldn't I?

Back to the mythical Otari MX-5050.

"I met a kid who needed an eight-track and gear, as I was moving out of my storage space in Atlanta in 2020," Robert tells me.

I responded, shocked, "The kid got the Otari?!"

"Yes!" Robert shoots back. "It was really amazing, actually!"

I am incredulous. "The kid has the machine that the big albums were made on?!"

"Yes! I signed it for him!" Robert replies. "It was pure synchronicity magic. The artifact is now refurbished and running in his own Michigan home studio!"

Upon reflection, I find it charming that Robert gave the Otari away, like some kind of gesture of thanks to the universe for the good fortune the machine brought him. However, at the time, this exchange made me furious!

Speaking of furious . . .

Pt. Two: "The Cymbal Crash for Hilarie"

This passage is about the intensity Robert and Hilarie both brought to the studio, Robert's granular memory of production and engineering detail, and how the creative process can bring out bad behavior in reasonable people.

"On *Fun Trick Noisemaker*," Robert says, "Hilarie was the main visionary with me. That was like *our* album."

"We set up at Kyle's house after we left California so we could continue working," Hilarie recalls. "We were recording the crash cymbal on 'She's Just Like Me,' and I had an idea of how it would sound best."

On the occasion of the thirtieth anniversary of the release of *Fun Trick Noisemaker*, musician John Ferguson—Robert formed the Apples side project Ulysses with John in 2002, and John became a member of the Apples in 2006 after Hilarie's departure—posted the following on Facebook:

"One time, in 2006, Beck and his band played a secret show right after our performance at a club in DC. Before the show, backstage, the guys in Beck's band were raving to Robert about *Fun Trick Noisemaker*, particularly the crash cymbal in 'She's Just Like Me.'"

This struck me as a very specific detail to reference on a deep cut, but when you listen to the song, the reason behind Beck's band being enamored of it is clear. The particular repeated cymbal sound throughout the chorus of "She's Just

Like Me" feels similar to the repeated across-the-screen wipe transitions in *Star Wars* that take us from sinister darkness to sun-drenched desert.

This feeling is a microcosm of the artistic dichotomy that existed between Robert and Hilarie while she was still in the band, and especially on this record that, according to Robert, was a shared vision.

I was compelled to investigate. I did not expect the emotional content.

Apple Picking, Pt. Two
"She's Just Like Me" from *Fun Trick Noisemaker*

My inquiry started with innocent prodding, but I quickly realized I felt guilty for poking.

Robert's answers on a technical topic seem to be woven into lingering emotions. We stop short of venturing into the personal dynamic of Robert and Hilarie as partners, but there is plenty to glean from the passion in the exchange about percussion.

> *Turn your eyes away from here*
> *She yearns to fly away from here*
> —"She's Just Like Me"

Again, if it brings you closer to the music, that is what we are here for.

Hilarie: "I had been doing a lot of psychedelic cymbal stuff in Secret Square (Hilarie's side project with musician Lisa Janssen) and experimenting with alternate mic placements, mainly from underneath."

"I felt I knew it best, and I'd been spending time under

my cymbal putting in this work," she continues. "Robert refused and said we were going to mic it his way. I wouldn't give up until we got into a stupid argument about it. I was stubborn and petulant and didn't want to give up. Finally, Robert got his way. So he thought."

Knowing I was going to get Robert's take on this, when I read Hilarie's explanation, it sounded slightly like fighting words to me. Justifiable fighting words, considering what I know of Robert's insistent working process, but fighting words nonetheless.

I was a little nervous!

"We were talking through the talkback mic, but Robert couldn't see me," Hilarie explains, recalling the session.

Most modern recording studio layouts allow the engineer to see the musicians, but not at Kyle's house, a reality that Hilarie used to her advantage.

"While Robert got ready, I set the mic in that sweet spot under the cymbal where I wanted it. I tracked the cymbal, and we listened back in the control room. Robert was like, 'Whoa! This sounds amazing!' Totally happy. I gloated. 'Ha-ha, I moved the mic to where I wanted it to be!'"

So sneaky for the sake of art. I approve, and Hilarie's admission that she "gloated" motivates me to push for a similar confession from Robert later.

"Robert was furious with me as a matter of principle, because he won the argument and I did my thing anyway," Hilarie says. "He eventually got over it, but so many people comment on that cymbal crash."

Hilarie concludes matter-of-factly, "I knew that cymbal so well. Of course I should have been the one miking it!"

Again, I was nervous about asking Robert for his response to this. However, I find nerves motivating, not debilitating.

Robert's initial response was slightly self-effacing coupled with a solidly held stance. Frankly, an excellent example of world-class diplomacy . . . at first.

Robert: "It's an interesting recollection that highlights her contending with me in the studio. My recollection has always been how she made that amazing cymbal sound. I always loved it. I think that different people remember things in the way that reflects their personalities, maybe."

Hmm, slightly self-effacing coupled with a crumbling solidly held stance now mixed with subtle shade. What had I gotten myself into?

Robert continues, and this is when I start to feel weird, but also start to become fascinated with the display of artistic passion over one cymbal sound on one thirty-year-old song. "I always bragged about that cymbal," he says. "For her, she beat me. My memory has always been of her innovative engineering moment on our album. It sounded great from below, which is how we did it. Her idea!"

I asked again if Hilarie is correct to characterize Robert as "furious," not to create a "gotcha" moment with my subject, but just the opposite. I want a "get him" moment that allows listeners to begin to "get" Robert as a more emotionally complex producer and songwriter whose work is not as singularly sunny as it has been portrayed for decades.

She's just like me
But she can see
The sad faces
She knows they're there
She's always aware
Of empty spaces
—"She's Just Like Me"

Yes. I am trying to persuade you to listen to this fantastic song.

"It's part of the writing of songs for us," Robert explained to *Tape Op* at the end of his interview in 1996. When Robert wrote songs, he was doing so with ideas about the production techniques he would apply to them and the equipment he would need, already in mind.

"I had never used these kinds of pieces of gear, even though I told the record label that I had so they would give us a budget," Robert admits.

These sounds were already part of the songs that he heard in his head. So what if he had to lie to bring them to life?

Listen to "She's Just Like Me," and you will hear no lies, only truth. The song is sad, just one of many songs by the Apples that go against stereotype, as we will see, but "She's Just Like Me" is not the same song without this cymbal sound. I understand why Beck's band was taken with it, and I understand why Robert and Hilarie fought over it.

Robert: "We hardly even knew how to engineer then—it was more like we were trying to figure out what was good and maybe it was more heated for one than the other of us."

"I'm sure we may have argued," he admits. "It was not an uncommon feature of our relationship, and that is not always helpful in the studio. But what she remembers as laughing in my face, I always remember as me rushing into the drum room and being like, 'Wow, it sounds really great!'"

When you give someone the keys to your emotional kingdom and they undermine your confidence, it is one of the most awful things that can happen to a person, especially a vulnerable person, like an artist tends to be.

I am not a marriage counselor after the fact. I am illustrating the intense working dynamic at play that resulted in records that have stood the test of time. Robert's insight shapes a deeper understanding of the work.

Robert and I went off the record at this point because the discussion was about to become more about Robert and Hilarie's marriage than about their music. He warned me that I probably didn't want to dig deeper.

Then, almost a month later, unprompted, Robert returned to the story. "I don't want to appear free from blame for being annoyed as I had recollected before. Memory sort of keeps clarifying itself—Hilarie's perspective is right in that maybe I was somewhat annoyed as well as overjoyed."

As if to deflect from this emotional admission, Robert begins to nerd out with a technical breakdown from his perspective that is pure Robert Schneider, producer at your service. Please remember, this is a level of detail thirty years removed. Not about an album, not about a song, not about a drum track . . . this is about one cymbal crash.

"I will tell you more about that cymbal crash," Robert begins.

The details contained in the following explanation may make you feel like you are reading an issue of *Modern Drummer*. This is exactly why I am including them here, not only for nerds like me, but for Beck's band members whose curiosity about the "She's Just Like Me" cymbal crash initiated this conversation in the first place.

"I was very happy with the overall crash and was elated with Hilarie's mic placement," Robert says, setting the scene. "However, the reason I wanted the microphone above the cymbal was because that particular cymbal generated a very deep bass tone underneath it. Some large cymbals do that."

I tend to make a mental note when I see a drum setup that is atypical, and Hilarie tended to use what I call "a giant crash cymbal."

"Hilarie uses a twenty-inch crash ride, or bigger," Robert confirms. "That one may have been twenty-four-inch. I had to go to great lengths to eliminate the hum from it, which was weird because we had moved the mic above the cymbal."

As usual, Robert's memory of what happened next begins with a positive frame.

"It was useful," he says. "I learned how to use the EQ better and experimented with phase cancellation and compression. It was a struggle to cut the hum without making the cymbal sound thin, but it worked out great. I finally got it! It sounded so good!"

Still, it seems like even now, Robert continues to hear the hum of Hilarie's giant crash ride in his mind.

"It was surprising. I couldn't hear the hum with my ear in the control room from above, but apparently the microphone picked it up. It was an SM57, not a fancy mic, but remember, I was not an engineer then."

Yes, I remember. Go on.

"We got the take, and it sounded totally amazing. I was so happy when I rushed in to tell Hilarie it was done. However, perhaps I was maybe a little annoyed when I saw the microphone underneath the cymbal."

I laugh out loud as I imagine Robert running into the room and stopping short in his tracks when, after all that, he sees the microphone moved from where he placed it. His half-hearted "However, perhaps I was maybe a little annoyed," is one of the most controlled descriptions of anger I have ever heard.

"We had this whole big conversation about it—an argument according to her story—because I had to struggle to correct it," he says.

Robert was right to be annoyed, then and now, and I feel a little bad for laughing, but pushing for the truth behind the recording deepens the legacy of the work, so I do.

"The mic had been placed back into the zone where the cymbal hummed. That's why I was struggling. But it sounded amazing! I was always happy with it, and I have told the story of Hilarie's engineering innovation ever since. It was a great move to put the mic there. It made a unique sound, and I have even used the technique again with cymbals that do not hum!"

I like that Robert adds the "that do not hum!" at the end there. This story is clearly still so visceral for him.

And then he adds . . .

"I am okay with 'furious.' Please use that word."

The following reads like a confession and validates this entire inquiry with words that say so much about Robert's art, about artists, and, frankly, about people in general.

"I am perceived as 'Mr. Nice,'" he says. "I'm not necessarily. I believe in humanity's ambition to be good, but no one is nice!"

Robert continues, "If you are characterized as being 'nice' too often, by too many people, it raises a red flag! It indicates that maybe the person you're talking about is either used to showing you that version of themselves or you haven't dug deep enough.

"I don't want to be scary," Robert concludes. "I would harm no one ever. I want to be real, and for history, I want to be 'furious,' not 'gentle.'"

"I am filled with fire."

5. "ALL THREE": THE SONGWRITING OF THE APPLES IN STEREO

"Pop is what you see on TV," Robert said to me during our conversation about the Apples playing the part of "pop," the Olivia Tremor Control filling the role of "art," and Neutral Milk Hotel as "deep" in the Elephant 6 dynamic.

"We were all three," he says.

"If you're on TV, you're a simplified cartoon character," Robert elaborated in *Endless Endless*. "You're not the subtle artist anymore, regardless of who you really are."

Reading this last comment made me feel sad.

The Apples in Stereo really are "all three" as Robert claims. Their catalog has a greater range than what has been said about the band would suggest, including what has been said about the band, by the band.

Would the Apples be so easily and incorrectly labeled "sunny" forever if their catalog had not existed as part of the "sunny" section in the imaginary Elephant 6 box set? If it ever does exist, please package it in a trunk for pun fans!

Before my memories about the Pet Sounds studio were clarified with visual and other sensory confirmations, I wondered if I had recalled the room being so dark because it actually was, or maybe I only remembered it this way because of the records that were made there.

The Beach Boys album *Pet Sounds* that gave the studio its name has dark underpinnings that are not immediately evident to the casual listener. Less than ten seconds into the opening cut "Wouldn't It Be Nice," Brian Wilson sings, "Wouldn't it be nice to live together in the kind of world where we belong?" meaning we currently live in the kind of world where we *don't* belong.

Brian's explanation that the song is about "the need to have the freedom to live with somebody" only underscores the controlling and abusive relationship that Brian still had with his father at the time, even at twenty-three years old. In retrospect, it is profound that we can hear the origins of the persistent mental health issues that occupied Brian for the rest of his life.

Brian Wilson is Robert's musical hero, and the Beach Boys is his favorite band, so it isn't a stretch to look at Robert's songs through the lens of someone who covers up dark pain with dazzling production. Like Brian, Robert uses the studio as a sacred instrument. I am still impressed that Robert admitted to being "furious" about having his microphone moved!

When Robert receives that backhanded compliment "mad genius," which typically mentions Brian Wilson and the Beach Boys in the same breath, he counters by explaining that the Apples—like his second-favorite band, the Beatles—were a team.

Still, it is Robert who is at the controls, creating the perception that this Pink Floyd–christened band exists at the heart of the sun when so much that was captured on tape lives on the dark side of the moon.

That word "dark" is not associated with the Apples in

Stereo. Like, ever.

When I use the word "dark" to describe the band's music, it is "I Am the Walrus" and "Strawberry Fields Forever" by Robert's second-favorite band that are in the front of my mind. I was literally frightened by these John Lennon masterpieces when I was a child, and I am literally frightened by them as an adult too.

As author Adam Clair recalls in *Endless Endless*, during an uncharacteristic run of solo shows in 2011, Jeff Mangum was asked by an audience member what his favorite song was. His answer of "I Am the Walrus" aligns all too well with the surrealistic chaos, disrupted nostalgia, and existential unease heard in the sonic world Robert created for *In the Aeroplane Over the Sea*.

"I get lots of love from the public, and within the collective, but they don't see the thoughtfulness and creativity that I have put into these projects," Robert confides. "They don't listen to the lyrics. They don't see how sensitive or earnest or personally deep I was."

I wrestled with including that quote from Robert because I don't believe he is complaining, even if it might sound like it.

What I hear is an artist frustrated by decades of being misunderstood and having that misunderstanding compounded by all the other roles, responsibilities, and repercussions that he had to take on, live up to, and, later, come to terms with.

Eric says, "If my songwriting is a kitchen faucet that has been left on halfway, Robert's songwriting is the inner-city fire hydrant that has been opened." His metaphor has a double meaning about Robert turning on the waterworks.

"They are melancholy songs," Robert tells me. "Most of

my songs are sad."

Often stormy instead of sunny, summery, or sweet, Robert's sad songs that you still sing along to can also turn scary and severe.

So much artistic intensity was compressed through the electronic wiring of Pet Sounds during the brief time the studio existed. The emotional intensity coursing through the physical wiring of the artists who worked there has yet to be fully understood.

Hearts and promises were broken in this room. A closer examination of the songs reveals more of who the artists really are.

Apple Picking, Pt. Three
"Benefits of Lying (With Your Friend)" from *Her Wallpaper Reverie*

"Mike Watt is the model to me of what a rock musician should be like," Robert says after I bring up a show I attended in 1986 when I was only fourteen. The iconic bassist's post-Minutemen band Firehose was opening for Sonic Youth at Irving Plaza in downtown Manhattan, and I had arrived early. Mike was hanging out and wandering around in the audience area of the venue.

Robert remembers, "When Jeff lived with us, he saw Mike play at the Mercury Cafe in Denver. Jeff was so charged up when he came back. He told me that, after the show, Mike came off the stage and just hung out, hugging everybody and chatting with them, like he was one of the crowd."

"That image, the hero stepping off the stage and hugging all of the kids, made an impact on me," Robert shares. "I relate to Mike a lot. When we were younger, I used to go off and hang out with kids that I met, but then sometimes I would be late for the show because I'd be playing video games in their apartments."

Recalling our similar Mike Watt stories about him hanging out with the audience reminded me of a video I saw on TikTok of a young Apples fan named Izzy covering "Benefits of Lying (With Your Friend)" from the *Her Wallpaper Reverie* EP, released in 1999.

This kid clearly was not even alive when the song was released, and he probably was a toddler when the Apples in Stereo last toured, but his connection with Robert's sensitivity is clear in the performance.

The kid's subtle vocal performance relates the quiet candor of the lyrics and takes the song to a place that makes you feel like what made Jeff Mangum feel so "charged up" by meeting Mike Watt that night in Denver.

Everything I say falls away
Like the fade on the radio song
And everything I try passed me by
Like the tide seems to rise, then it's gone

Hearing the kid perform the song acoustically is not the pop we "see on TV" at all. In fact, his cover version reveals more about the writer than the writer's full-band version does.

Robert adds swirling production touches to the original that are fine, but that do not serve the feelings of disconnection he is expressing in the lyrics as well as no swirls would. Even for Brian Wilson, mastering the balance between the vulnerability of a song against potentially masking that vulnerability with production is quite a challenge.

> *Sometimes when I'm by myself*
> *I can't find myself*
> *And there's no one there*
> —"Benefits of Lying (With Your Friend)"

Robert pulls back on the bells and whistles when the tune arrives at this refrain, but the moment needs to play even starker. The kid on TikTok knows what to do.

This is one of Robert's saddest moments in song.

Without knowing it, the kid calls Robert out for obscuring his feelings, and I am glad he does because even at two million plays on Spotify, there is a bigger audience waiting for the writer of "Benefits of Lying (With Your Friend)" to offer them a Mike Watt–style hug.

Apple Picking, Pt. Four
"Please" from *Velocity of Sound*

"It was my goal for the record to sound like the speakers were blown."

When I ask the band to name a few tunes from the Apples catalog that immediately come to mind, Eric responds, "Please," which is polite, and also one of the band's songs, so that worked out.

I made the mistake of reading the 2002 *Pitchfork* review of *Velocity of Sound*, the album that opens with "Please," before writing about the song. That piece was published during the years when *Pitchfork* was best known for intentionally trying to trigger readers.

It is amusing that the review accuses the Apples of "milking the preferences of their newly acquired audience" with *Velocity of Sound*. This is in reference to how the band's song "Signal in the Sky (Let's Go!)" was included on *Heroes & Villains: Music Inspired by the Powerpuff Girls*, an official soundtrack released in 2000 for the popular animated TV series, which aired on the Cartoon Network for six seasons.

"Signal in the Sky" was later included in the "Superfriends" episode of the program, which was based on the song's lyrics. The Apples showed up for a cameo, and a video for the song featuring characters from the series aired at the end.

The Apples then released the *Let's Go!* EP in the summer of 2001. Unlike earlier EPs, this one comes off like the record label taking advantage of a marketing opportunity, but at the end of the day the band approved it.

In their review of the EP *Pitchfork* declared, "The Apples in Stereo are now a children's band," and this snarky attitude clearly had staying power that made its way into the 2002 *Velocity of Sound* review.

The criticism had unintended staying power for Robert as well. Seven years later, in 2009, he *did* release a children's album under the name Robbert Bobbert and the Bubble Machine. Robbert Bobbert was even briefly scheduled to become an animated series produced by Puny Entertainment, the studio known for *Yo Gabba Gabba!*

Hey, I said this chapter is about artistic range!

Seriously, offering "Signal in the Sky (Let's Go!)" to *The Powerpuff Girls* show, releasing the *Let's Go!* EP, and the subsequent visibility for the Apples surrounding both, amounts to nothing more than a rising artist accepting a career opportunity. In this case, it was an opportunity that did not diverge from the band's values, and it was one that they were excited to be a part of.

Ultimately, the commercial success of the song surpassed critical skepticism when "Signal in the Sky" also appeared in an ad for Samsung cell phones. We will discuss how this commercial use and other lucrative opportunities to use songs by the Apples in Stereo to advertise global bands affected their career in chapter 8.

The downside of aligning with corporate entities, be they television networks or cell phone networks, is that while it may not necessarily take away from establishing the perception of the band's catalog as living in the artistically substantial light that it deserves, it doesn't work toward it either, as proved by the press treating the Apples like easy targets.

Professional decisions always have the potential to alienate fans and critics, but they also have the potential to create a greater awareness of the artist. We will continue to discuss questionable career choices, but the point of this particular story is: The insinuation that Robert was motivated to milk anything other than his muse for *Velocity of Sound* is not only amusing, it is laughable.

"I got a call from Jeff Price," Robert recalls. You will remember Jeff Price as the cofounder of SpinART Records, the label that released *Velocity of Sound* and one of the people who has seen Robert pissed. "*Velocity of Sound* had a strong single, 'Please.' It did pretty well!" Robert says. "Jeff was in his car and had just popped in the master of the record. He called me in a panic . . ."

"'Robert! There's something wrong with the master! It

sounds like my car stereo speakers are blown. We have to do something!'" Robert recalls Jeff yelling through the phone.

"Jeff's poor heart must have sunk really low at that moment when I explained to him that it was my goal for the record to sound like the speakers were blown."

Hearts and promises were broken in this car!

"Please" flaunts a side of Robert's production powers that go back to the idea of incorporating the sound of the studio into the songwriting. Unlike "Benefits of Lying (With Your Friend)," "Please" is not especially notable for Robert's lyricism, but it is notable for his aggressive, hyper-melodious production-driven technique, and is proud of it.

Velocity of Sound is a brutal-sounding record in the best way, and "Please" is a single cut from the torn denim of "Judy Is a Punk" and "I Wanna Be Sedated."

"The Ramones were the number one influence on *Velocity of Sound*," Robert confirms. "Seeing *Rock 'n' Roll High School* as a little kid was one of the things that made me want to be a musician."

"We were going for a record that is great in the way the first Ramones album is," Eric agrees. "*Velocity of Sound* is the Apples deciding to do an album that is stripped down and sounds the way we play live: fast, fuzzy, and distorted."

After a count-in, buzzsaw guitars compressed to hell are matched with Hilarie's "put-the-drumstick-through-the-drumhead" snare sound. It sounds like an assault. Although Robert's airy voice isn't anything like Joey Ramone's, if we could put the Apples on the CBGB stage in 1976 playing "Please," the walls would sweat. Robert said earlier that he doesn't like his own voice, but when it is paired with Hilarie's as she comes in on the second verse, they sound perfect together.

Go ahead and call the Apples out for participating in a cable television cartoon, but "Please" acknowledge that this same band seeks to throw the TV off the balcony into the hotel pool too.

Apple Picking, Pt. Five
"Stream Running Over" from *The Discovery of a World Inside the Moone*

In the summer of 2023, Robert came to New York City to participate in a Q&A and perform some Apples songs acoustically at the IFC Center in Manhattan following a screening of *The Elephant 6 Recording Co.* documentary.

He explains to the audience that the Apples toured without set lists and would call out the next song when they finished the last song.

"I still like to do that, so I haven't planned what I'm going to play," he tells the crowd.

When an audience member shouts out a request for "Stream Running Over," it seems like Robert is quickly applying his mathematical mind to the performance he is about to do in that he looks like he is literally loading the song into his consciousness.

"Okay, 'Stream Running Over,' yes—let's see how that's gonna go."

As it appears on the Apples in Stereo album *The Discovery of a World Inside the Moone*, "Stream Running Over" plays as a propulsive indie rocker bookended by psychedelic guitars.

The insistent backbeat is augmented by killer handclaps that highlight the funky edge that is a hallmark of this record. That funk sound is most prevalent on the single "The Bird That You Can't See," which we will discuss in the following chapter.

Once I cut my hand, but the wound was not part of me
Well, now I'm a man, there's a wound at the heart of me
—"Stream Running Over"

Robert's image of injury as irrelevant is powerful. Our bodies are only vessels subject to the dangerous will of the world, and while we can feel physical pain, our being, our soul, is forever resilient.

The "wound at the heart" of the "man" is the compass we live by. The "wound" represents the compassion and empathy that allows us to harness cosmic pain and alleviate the suffering of others.

The sensitivity of "Stream Running Over" on the album version of the song is not as shrouded as it is on "Benefits of Lying (With Your Friend)," but it still doesn't touch what Robert quickly pulls out of himself at the IFC Center in the summer of 2023.

I think about how Robert had just watched his best friend Bill Doss moments before, larger than life on-screen, just over a decade since his passing, and how this acoustic performance of "Stream Running Over" feels like Robert is wearing the weary wisdom that comes with loss.

Notably, the *Let's Go!* EP mentioned previously—the label promo tool that annoyed *Pitchfork*—contained an acoustic demo of "Stream Running Over" that, when compared to Robert's 2023 performance in NYC, is like listening to two different tunes.

Robert would go on to perform "Stream Running Over" again at the memorial concert in Athens for his best friend Will Hart, following Will's passing less than two years later.

●

Apple Picking, Pt. Six
"Where We Meet" from *Velocity of Sound*
"I'm playing a lot of drums these days and loving it!"

I was excited to hear this from Hilarie after she mentioned "Where We Meet," a deep cut by the Apples that I didn't know, but immediately fell in love with when I heard its astonishing sing-along melody.

Hilarie doesn't play drums as much these days because she is the front person, along with her husband Per Ole Bratset, who is also a songwriter and guitarist, in the High Water Marks. The band is based in Grøa, a small village in western Norway roughly halfway between Bergen and Trondheim, where Hilarie has lived for over a decade.

Hilarie is an absolute weapon on drums throughout *Velocity of Sound*.

The record represents the summation of her powers as a founding member of the Apples in Stereo, and her performances on "Where We Meet," "Please," and "I Want," one of her originals that we will discuss later, bring me back to that nagging feeling about *New Magnetic Wonder* and *Travellers in Space and Time* lacking Hilarie's presence.

Even though Hilarie plays on *New Magnetic Wonder*, when I ask her about the experience of making the album, she replies, "I mean, I don't know. I was left out of a lot of what happened on that record."

Robert and Hilarie broke up before the recording of *New Magnetic Wonder*, so it is easy to imagine their already-tense relationship adding new pressure to the sessions. Five years earlier, however, Hilarie was locked in and ready to rock on *Velocity of Sound*.

Hilarie's snare hits on "Where We Meet" are instantly recognizable, which also goes to show how adept Robert had become at getting her sound. I have heard no word on whether Hilarie dared to move any cymbal mics this time!

"She was like thunder onstage," Robert says. "Epic."

Robert continues, "I love that song. It's about . . . well, maybe I shouldn't tell you. 'Where We Meet' is very mysterious."

This out-of-character coy moment lasts for six weeks, and then Robert finishes his thought, explaining that the subject matter involves a topic often discussed around these pages.

"'Where We Meet' is about being a cat, or, rather, it identifies being cats with being kids, with freedom," he says. "But that meaning is obscured . . . secret. Well, if you listen to it and imagine that it's about being a cat, then it's kind of obvious."

It is notable on "Where We Meet," and all of *Velocity of Sound*, that amid the intentional torrent of distortion, Eric's bass gets much more room to play and often carries the melody.

"Up until *Velocity of Sound*, the goal had always been aiming at pop perfection with the sort of production that is very much a studio construct à la Brian Wilson and Phil Spector," Eric says.

"Without Robert needing to carve out space for a lush pop arrangement, my bass line had no musical toes to step on!"

Eric continues, "I love 'Where We Meet.' I can't think of a previous song of Robert's with the rhythmic chord bombs that he drops instead of chords that just follow his melody. John and Robert are mostly just playing those chords, so there is space for my bass line as a melody."

This chapter has been about what the Apples songs actually are versus what they have long been perceived to be, and "Where We Meet" becomes evidence in the case for the Apples as a guitar band with its ripping solo from Robert.

"It's one of my favorite solo melodies," he says.

Somewhat hilariously, as I chide him for not taking enough credit for numerous artistic and career accomplishments, it is Robert's guitar playing that he feels most cheated about.

"Baby boomers worship every goddamn person that ever touched the instrument," he shouts over text, clearly worked up. "That is my gripe! There aren't even that many guitar heroes in my whole generation. I feel like I got robbed!"

I know Robert is half-joking with the self-stroking, but his solo on "Where We Meet" is a screamer that also benefits from his "blow out Jeff Price's car speakers" style of production.

When I ask for the best example of Robert's guitar heroism, he points me to the solo on "I Can't Believe" (from *The Discovery of a World Inside the Moone*) as being "more *Guitar Hero*–type fare."

This song was mentioned earlier as one that contains Robert's "secret trick" of adding a Moog MG-1 synthesizer playing the same riff as the guitars.

"I'm telling you this with some sense of embarrassment," Robert admits. "Because of the other things that I do musically, including bass on Neutral Milk Hotel and the Olivia Tremor Control, the only instrument that I actually play well was overlooked."

I will leave the responsibility of making Robert a guitar god to musicians more qualified than me.

I am with him on the use of the word "overlooked,"

however. Please revisit the songs we have discussed in this chapter and listen to the others that we are about to. The Apples in Stereo catalog reveals a pop band that is also "art" and "deep." The Apples in Stereo are "all three."

6. STRICTLY KNOWN AS FUZZ AND PRE: JOHN HILL & ERIC ALLEN

"I t's a completely different band each time."

John Hill is telling me about how the Apples in Stereo morph from record to record. "Each one is its own thing," he says. This is not untrue. If it were, I wouldn't have so confidently told Robert in chapter 1 that the version of the band consisting of John, Eric, Hilarie, and Robert was THE version. My mind has not changed seventy-five pages later.

"Thirty-seven people have been in this band over the years," fictional metal icon David St. Hubbins famously recalls in the film *This Is Spinal Tap*, and while the Apples don't go quite that far, according to the band's Wikipedia page, the current and former membership does go exactly to eleven. No kidding.

In addition to all the Apples already mentioned, musician Chris McDuffie was also a full-time member on keyboards from 1999 to 2002, and he appeared in some of the band's most iconic publicity photos.

"Chris was my main studio partner on *Discovery* and *Wallpaper*," Robert says.

Eric Allen joined the Apples after the release of *Fun Trick*

Noisemaker in 1995, making him and John Hill the only members of the band besides Robert to reach the thirty-year mark, playing all the way to the end, if there ever really is an end. Spoiler: There is no end. "The Music Never Stopped," like the Grateful Dead said. Read on.

Official promotional photo of the Apples in Stereo from the Her Wallpaper Reverie *era. (L–R): Chris McDuffie, Eric Allen, John Hill, Hilarie Sidney, Robert Schneider. Photo by Richard Alden Peterson.*

"We spent two weeks in Glendora, California, doing the basic tracks, and once we came home, we moved it into Kyle Jones's house," John recalls.

While Robert says that he and Hilarie were the main artistic visionaries on *Fun Trick Noisemaker*, John was Robert's primary partner at Kyle's studio, which Robert had now named Pet Sounds.

"I was with Robert almost every day during *Fun Trick Noisemaker*," John recalls.

I hope that "almost" means John missed the controversial cymbal-microphone-moving mess.

Since John was brought into the band by Hilarie, and she and Robert were the driving artistic forces behind *Fun Trick Noisemaker*, John felt that his consistent presence might have been too much.

"I think it kind of strained my relationship with Hilarie, but actually I was just making myself useful," John says.

"Making that album was the beginning of us using semipro recording gear, and there was always something to fix. I was a fairly basic guitarist back then, compared to Robert, so in my mind I was making up for it in other ways."

John adds, "Robert had way more musical experience, but I had way more life experience. If I hadn't been there, I can guarantee we would have been late to every show, if we made it at all. To be honest, from the early days, I kind of thought of myself as less of an asset musically and more helpful in getting things done."

John might be being modest.

Robert takes a temporary break from strict nicknaming to say, "John's songwriting contributions to the Apples have always been as 'the Riffmaster.' 'The Riffmaster' is like 'the Beastmaster,' except you get to wear jeans instead of a fur tunic."

During the early *Fun Trick Noisemaker* sessions in California, Robert remembers a songwriting session in which John changed the course of the band's song "Innerspace."

"We stayed up all night working through the guitar parts," Robert recalls. "At that point, there was only the main riff that evolved, not the chorus melody. As John and I were playing together, he suddenly reversed the order of the two chords. It was magical."

John is credited as the cowriter of "Innerspace," and the song is now the second-most popular track by the Apples in

Stereo on Spotify with over five million streams.

Remember the *Heroes & Villains: Music Inspired by the Powerpuff Girls* soundtrack we discussed a few pages ago that the Apples appeared on? The one that caused a crisis for that one *Pitchfork* critic? The Elephant 6–associated band Dressy Bessy also appears on that soundtrack (as does Bill Doss of the Olivia Tremor Control).

This photo of the Apples in Stereo, taken during the era of The Discovery of a World Inside the Moone, *is my personal favorite. Hilarie looks pissed, Robert's eyes look like slits, and I am envious of the hair on Chris. (L–R): Hilarie Sidney, Robert Schneider, Eric Allen, Chris McDuffie, John Hill. Photo by Richard Alden Peterson..*

Dressy Bessy is John Hill's band with his partner Tammy Ealom. Tammy formed the band in 1996, and John joined in 1997.

Like so many acts with connections to Elephant 6 during

the days when the collective was beginning to boil over, after John joined Dressy Bessy following the release of *Fun Trick Noisemaker*, his status as a guitarist in the Apples in Stereo meant that Dressy Bessy was immediately lumped into the collective.

As John recalls in *Endless Endless*, "Tammy didn't want that, and I didn't want it, either. Dressy Bessy really didn't have much of a relationship to Elephant 6. It was just Tammy's band, and I just happened to be in it."

I have been wondering if the "all three" qualities of the Apples would be more apparent if the band had formed in a world where Elephant 6 never existed, drawing in fans with their seemingly straightforward pop and keeping them with their psychedelic substance(s).

Dressy Bessy, on the other hand, was always a candy band. This is not a criticism. This is a feature. Palettes change, but candy is forever, and Dressy Bessy was always a bit too sweet for the 6.

Because of this, Dressy Bessy benefited from *The Powerpuff Girls* association in a way the Apples couldn't. The band is named after a Playskool toy doll, after all, and Tammy's songs are unapologetically cheerful, optimistic, and fun.

No critic could accuse Dressy Bessy of becoming a children's band because the songs already chewed bubblegum like a charismatic brat who sticks it under the desk. John bounced around at stage right with the Apples, but with Dressy Bessy he took that upbeat posture closer to front and center.

His joyful stage presence perfectly countered Tammy's gravely streetwise riot grrrl of the Rocky Mountains vocals— think peak Go-Go's-era Belinda Carlisle and Jane Wiedlin as one person. With plenty of pop hooks, Dressy Bessy looked less like an Apples side project for John and more like his only band to Dressy Bessy fans.

"Many people don't get that Dressy Bessy is its own thing," John says. I feel his frustration. Even as a casual observer, I often thought of John as having two bands. "We share some Elephant 6 fans, but most Dressy Bessy fans either don't know I'm in the Apples or have never even heard of the Apples."

I don't take what John says as a comment on the popularity of the Apples. Instead, it is confirmation that John managed to be in two different bands at once with two different fan bases.

"People we've worked with in the music business have treated Dressy Bessy as an extension of the Apples," John explains, "but it's not true." Just prior to Dressy Bessy appearing on *The Powerpuff Girls* soundtrack, the band was offered an opportunity that is still paying off over twenty-five years later.

The 1999 teen comedy film about queer love, *But I'm a Cheerleader*, starring the generally adored actor Natasha Lyonne, has become an important touchstone in the gay community.

Natasha has seen a major career resurgence recently, first with her breakout return in *Orange Is the New Black* for Netflix, followed by cocreating *Russian Doll* for the network, and culminating with major award nominations for the Peacock show *Poker Face*. This has helped *Cheerleader* continue to be handed down throughout the years, with the film becoming even more foundational for questioning youth every time it is.

The two songs by Dressy Bessy that appear in the movie

and are key to its narrative— "Just Like Henry" and "If You Should Try to Kiss Her," both from 1999's *Pink Hearts Yellow Moons* (yes, Lucky Charms cereal counts as candy!)—have now helped young people find Dressy Bessy for decades.

"*But I'm a Cheerleader* still brings in new fans," John confirms. "The movie has a life of its own and has gotten significantly more attention since the pandemic."

Additionally, Dressy Bessy songs were later featured in the hit TV show *Grey's Anatomy* (a medical drama that is the opposite of a superhero cartoon), and another film that became a cult hit, *She's the Man*.

Similar to how *Cheerleader* confronted sexual identity on the sidelines of team sports in 1999, *She's the Man* confronted gender roles on the field itself in 2006. In 2018, *Vice* called the film "The most important soccer movie of all time," proving its enduring influence on youth culture and, subsequently, continuing to put Dressy Bessy music in youthful ears.

A big difference between Dressy Bessy and the Apples in Stereo that also distanced the former from the ethos of Elephant 6 was how strategic Tammy has always been about being visible and image driven.

Where the Elephant 6 crowd was reclusive by nature, making the Apples appear to be the most media-friendly by default, Tammy was unabashed about keeping Dressy Bessy visually intriguing and accessible.

Similar to how Kurt Cobain played the game of artistic integrity versus commercial ambition—he famously wore a "Corporate Magazines Still Suck" T-shirt on the cover of *Rolling Stone*—in a much smaller yet still effective way, Dressy Bessy built an audience that, with the Apples on the rise at the same time, made the most modest member of the band its busiest.

"By 2005, Dressy Bessy was headlining the same clubs that the Apples were, but we were filling them with much different crowds," John says. "It was obviously a very exciting time as both of my bands picked up steam. There were a few years where I played over 200 shows."

He adds, "It was really fun, but I was always worrying about scheduling conflicts. I felt like I couldn't miss anything with either band. There were a few instances where dates had to be shuffled around or I had to rush from one tour to the next."

Here's John's entry to rival Robert sending off the *Velocity of Sound* tapes to be mixed in Brooklyn on the same day that he and Hilarie left Denver.

"We finished the studio recording of the 2003 self-titled Dressy Bessy album," John recalls, "and seven hours later I was flying to London to meet the Apples on tour."

Maybe John is just better at manifesting last-minute miracles.

Eight years earlier, just after the release of *Fun Trick Noisemaker*, the Apples embarked on their first major tour, opening for the Flaming Lips. Although Robert had started to acquire pro recording gear to continue building Pet Sounds, the band's touring rigs had yet to be upgraded.

On the way out of town to join the tour, the guitar pedal that provided John with his signature sound decided it would not be going with them.

"It crapped out on me, and I needed a fuzz pedal immediately," John recalls. "I found a Pro Co RAT pedal, but it was overly aggressive, so I called ProSound in Denver— this was before Guitar Center ever existed—and decided on a Danelectro Daddy O. When I came into the store and said to the salesman, 'I called about the fuzz pedal,' he shouted back, 'Johnny Fuzz!'"

John paid for the pedal and picked up his nickname for free.

He still has both.

Apple Picking, Pt. Seven
"The Bird That You Can't See" from *The Discovery of a World Inside the Moone*

"The *Fun Trick Noisemaker* sound covers the band all the way through *Her Wallpaper Reverie*," John comments about the stylistic shift that the Apples went through in 2000 to make *The Discovery of a World Inside the Moone*.

"Despite *Tone Soul Evolution* being a little slicker, it still fits. Then the sound took a turn with *Moone*, and I think 'The Bird That You Can't See' is a good example of that," he explains.

The song is a precursor to where the band would go on *Travellers in Space and Time* with the single "Dance Floor," which I am still questioning the artistic substance of as we near a critical evaluation of it. I remain committed to being open-minded!

I remember hearing "The Bird That You Can't See" for the first time shortly after *The Discovery of a World Inside the Moone* was completed. The funk of this cut took me by surprise but felt authentic because Robert doesn't go over the top in his writing, performance, or production.

If the track even so much as hinted at "Look! This white boy from South Africa can get funky!" it would fail in a spectacularly embarrassing way. Instead, Robert is completely convincing by leaning into the limits of his voice to offer up all of his soul and all of his love of an R&B edge.

"Hot-buttered" isn't Robert's strong suit, but the one he wears here fits well. The keyboard riff that permeates "The Bird That You Can't See" is Robert's hook. "That's a Roland Jupiter-6," he tells me. "I also had a few old Moogs in the studio. Roland and Moog have always been my go-to synthesizers. I also like Korg a lot!"

Hilarie lays it down on the Rogers Holiday "house kit" with much precision and no pretension. As John suggests, this is the first example of Robert's love of R&B starting to fully shine through, and Hilarie takes on the task like a session player under scrutiny. Hilarie mentions to me how producer Bryce Goggin was impressed by how perfectly she played to a click track during the production of *New Magnetic Wonder*, and I take note for listening later.

Twenty-five years removed from its initial release, "The Bird That You Can't See" doesn't sound current, and that is a compliment. It sounds even more straight out of the soul of the seventies than it did in 2000. Age helps the song play with a patina. In 2000, how hard would it be to imagine late-twenties Robert as a soul singer? Now it's easy.

John Hill's role as the logistical coordinator for the Apples when he wasn't performing on guitar carries through to this day, as he handles tour management for a handful of bands that revolve around Peter Buck (R.E.M.), Scott McCaughey (the Young Fresh Fellows, the Minus 5), and Steve Wynn (the Dream Syndicate), among others.

Dressy Bessy continues to perform and signed a record deal with Yep Roc in 2015, the same label that partnered with the Apples in Stereo and Elijah Wood to release *New*

Magnetic Wonder and *Travellers in Space and Time.*

"When *Fun Trick Noisemaker* was done, we began to look towards touring and knew we needed a permanent bass player," Robert remembers. "We had always wanted Eric to join the band, but he was too punk rock on guitar."

Robert's story reveals the source of Eric's nickname.

He is Punk Rock Eric: PRE.

I find it beautiful that Eric still signs his emails with his strict nickname, "PRE," as if to say, "Once an Apple, always an Apple."

"I wasn't even a fucking bass player! I was a guitar player who was totally wrong for the Apples. As a bass player, I was a blank slate," PRE says. As a result, Eric had fewer musical habits that were anathema to what the Apples were like in 1995.

"Learning by ear was how I became a guitarist. When I agreed to play with the Apples, I had the advantage of being roommates with an incredible bass player. Watching him play helped me shift my way of thinking away from guitar and to bass."

Robert was essentially Eric's other bass teacher. Eric says that, left to his own devices, the parts would have sounded like "Dee Dee Ramone on a bad day."

"When I joined, *Fun Trick Noisemaker* had just been released, so I played those bass lines," Eric explains. "If I had to write those parts, as a guitarist who had just picked up the bass, those songs wouldn't have that psychedelic yet Swiss watch quality that Robert had created."

Another effect that Eric had on the Apples in Stereo was personal.

"We liked and understood each other," he says. "As a band, and with the individual relationships we all had, and still have. Being able to travel together, to sleep in close quarters, and to live in the same impoverished condition in order to move our band forward is significant."

"We were poor, and had nothing, and it was the greatest," Eric remembers. "We knew we were doing something special. My feeling when I joined was *What could be better than playing in one of the greatest bands ever?*"

"When I was in high school, I read a quote from Paul Westerberg of the Replacements about starting a band," he continues. "Basically, Paul said 'Play with your friends because in the worst-case scenario, you still have your friends.' I love Fuzz, Hilarie, and Robert, maybe more now than I did back then, which really says something about how great they all are. I feel lucky to have found them, and I think they are lucky to have found me."

By the time the Apples recorded the Ramones-influenced *Velocity of Sound* seven years after Eric joined the band, he had far surpassed Dee Dee Ramone on bass. Eric also began contributing his own songs to the Apples at this time, making three writers in the band.

"PRE mostly makes experimental music, but he's a natural writer in a prose and poetry sense," Robert says of Eric, stopping short of temporarily re-nicknaming him "the Prosemaster."

"Robert started encouraging me to write once I was established in the band," Eric says. "My songs started with inspiration but became focused work. If something I write is going on an Apples album next to a song by Robert or Hilarie, I've got to give it my all."

"'Yore Days' is so beautiful," Robert says of this Eric

tune. "His lyrics are abstract, profound, and distinctive. I love it when he squeezes that voice into weird pop songs."

Is this the only band in history to contain three people named John? The Apples in Stereo as pictured during the Travellers in Space and Time *era. (L–R): Bill Doss, John Hill, John Dufilho, Robert Schneider, John Ferguson, Eric Allen. Photo by Adam Cantor.*

Robert points out this lyric from "Yore Days" as among the band's best:

> *Look on the page*
> *Where everybody wrote their names*
> *All of the lines are the same*
> *Is that what you want to be?*
> —"Yore Days" from *Velocity of Sound*

Robert says, "That lyric is so inspiring."

Eric continued to develop his songwriting voice, contributing "Next Year at About the Same Time" to *Travellers in Space and Time*. Bill Doss had become a permanent member of the Apples by then, and Eric asked him to take the lead vocal on the song.

No one knew that "Next Year" would be one of Bill's last lead vocal recordings before his untimely passing in 2012.

Look, I said I was going to give *Travellers in Space and Time* a chance. There is no need to gild the lily with sentimentality, but damn, I'm not crying, you're crying.

Apple Picking, Pt. Eight
"Next Year at About the Same Time" from *Travellers in Space and Time*
Eric says, "'Next Year at About the Same Time' is the song I wrote for the Apples that I am most proud of."

> *Four stoic trees spreading over woods*
> *White mossy fingers form a leafy hood*
> *Turning the night into some other life, now*
> —"Next Year at About the Same Time"

Even though the Apples in Stereo had officially expanded to a six-piece for *Travellers in Space and Time*, it is easy to imagine the "four stoic trees" that Eric writes about in this lyric as representing the Robert, Hilarie, John, and Eric dynamic that we have been discussing.

A "leafy hood" of lifted compatriots, traveling from town to town, performing under lights, and turning each night into this "some other life" as a band in a bonded caravan.

Or it could literally just be about nature. Eric's description of the making of the track lends weight to the former.

"Robert added a few touches that I hadn't anticipated that opened up the song, and I knew they were great. We went from a magician's clenched fist to an explosion of paper flowers and foam balls that initially seemed too much to have been held in one tight hand."

"I really labored over the lyrics," Eric continues. "Each verse translated visually in my mind as a clip from an unknown *cinema vérité* documentary, and this would not have been possible without Bill."

Eric's "cinema vérité" comment makes sense the moment you hear Bill's vocal, which sounds as if he is an obtuse observer of the scene Eric sets.

Eric considers himself an inhibited lead vocalist. "Bill's singing is the opposite of inhibited," he says of his late friend. "Knowing Bill would do all of the heavy lifting allowed me to work on the song without my usual limitations. He agreed to sing it without reservation."

Eric was smart to let Bill take the vocal on the song because, as he states, this unusual move gave Eric room to stretch on the bass part, and now gives this book a reference to Motörhead and, consequently, its first and only umlaut.

"With the bass higher in the mix, I could go for a strummy, Lemmy Kilmister sound, which I love but would have sounded ridiculous on an Apples song," Eric says.

Although he realized "Next Year" sounded different from any other Apples tune that had come before it, it is those differences that make the song interesting and, to my ears, a fitting tribute to Bill, however unintentional.

As promised, I have now begun to allow my coerced open mind to start being permeated by the last two Apples records.

I grew up reading *Modern Drummer* and dragging my mother to the drum center to sit there while I practiced by the hour. John Dufilho does his job here on drums, and there is no way I would throw shade at any drummer, but I still miss Hilarie.

My complaint is that I can literally hear what Hilarie would do on this track, and considering that she never had the opportunity to back up Bill Doss on a record, I am letting myself listen to the version of "Next Year at About the Same Time" that only my mind can play.

That said, the drum and keyboard pattern flourish throughout the song that is straight out of "Blue Jean" by David Bowie is a "great artists steal" moment that is worthy of recognition.

It is also notable that the "white mossy fingers" from the first verse changes to "dark mossy fingers" later in the song.

This feels important when watching a live performance of "Next Year at About the Same Time" from the band's set at the inaugural Starts with You Music & Arts Festival in Brazil on October 9, 2010. The Apples deliver a solid replication of the album version of the tune. Bill's vocal is especially powerful, making for an even more sobering listen considering he would be gone less than two years later.

7. "MAKE SURE EVERYONE KNOWS YOUR CONTRIBUTIONS": HILARIE SIDNEY

Don't be afraid to speak up and make sure you are heard. Be vocal. Be pushy.

—Hilarie Sidney

I ask Hilarie to talk to me about the issues girls face who want to join or start bands today, in an era when misogyny is on the rise again, and more specifically, when existing misogyny is being readily tolerated again.

How has this situation changed since the early nineties when Hilarie became a founding member of the Apples in Stereo and the Elephant 6 Recording Co.? How do girls avoid misogyny, and how do they deal with it when they don't? What happens when they can't get as many songs on the records, especially when it's not even on purpose, and just by default?

As a woman generating more art than ever during her fourth decade in rock, what does Hilarie say from this perspective of experience, success, and authority?

Hilarie is succinct: "Don't let anyone steal your ideas and make them their own."

This point is one I didn't think of. It is about men who

recognize a woman's genius, and instead of acknowledging and celebrating it, they claim it for themselves.

Hilarie Sidney in early-nineties Denver. "I remember buying that sepia film for my Olympus OM-10, so whoever took the picture was most likely using it." Courtesy of Hilarie Sidney.

Now it's Hilarie's turn to be furious.

"Just think about what Jann Wenner (the cofounder of *Rolling Stone*) said about why he didn't include Joni Mitchell in his book *The Masters*."

Jann stated that he left Joni out because he didn't view her as a "philosopher of rock and roll."

Hilarie says, "It's bullshit!"

Jann later went on to acknowledge that his comments were "inflammatory" and "badly chosen," which, to me, also sounds like bullshit. It sounds like a man being called out for being misogynistic and then trying to cover his ass.

Hilarie continues to drop essential advice: "Women have a leg up in the music business now compared to what it was like in the nineties, but it is still not a level playing field. It is still male-dominated. If you love what you're doing, do it, and do it with confidence. Don't let anyone walk over you, and don't let anyone tell you that you aren't good enough!"

Please note: This is not the Hilarie Sidney advocacy chapter. She doesn't need me or anyone for that. It is about Hilarie and her artistic achievements, but understanding her career means seeing it in the context of Hilarie as the only woman among the founding members of the Apples in Stereo and the Elephant 6 Recording Co. in early nineties America.

The subcontext of Hilarie's opening statement above, made more than thirty years after the fact, says what you think it says. I am grateful to be able to speak about Hilarie's fundamental importance to not only the scene and band she helped create and carry but also for women in music who have consistently been marginalized.

Hilarie puts it plainly: "It was a boys' club. Having been in the Apples and on the road since 1993, I started to have many more songs than could ever be released on an Apples record."

"After Robert and I got divorced, a lot of people . . . chose him over me," Hilarie said in a 2024 interview with *Chickfactor*, the influential fanzine founded in 1992—the same year as the Apples. "That's just the way it goes."

Yes, that *is* "just the way it goes," but it is not the way it *should* go.

In any story, the momentum of the narrative tends to dictate who the stars are, and as that story continues to get told and retold, the supporting characters tend to fade to the background until their vital support of the main players is forgotten about.

This reality hits me hard when I see Hilarie in promotional

posters for the Elephant 6 documentary. She is placed in the second row of people depicted in the film, as if to suggest that she is not as important to what is being promoted as the row of men in front of her are.

It hits me hard again when, in a conversation with one of the film's producers, Hilarie is referred to as a "lady from the scene." It hits me hard a third time when media coverage of a cultural movement that would not exist without her falls short of acknowledging that fact.

Oh, wow! I just realized that I sound like a curmudgeon who was raised by a feminist. Well, that's who I am. Seeking justified recognition is in my bones. I already did it for Robert, so don't be surprised! Fairly candid, but also fair. This is not a Hilarie Sidney advocacy chapter!

The woman doesn't even have a nickname as far as we know, and according to *The Elephant 6 Recording Co.* film, Hilarie lost a mail order or two in the early days when she was running the label in the most professional manner a group of dedicated unprofessionals could.

Remember: Robert said in chapter 4 that for *Fun Trick Noisemaker*, "Hilarie was the main visionary with me. That was like *our* album," a fact made abundantly clear in "the Great Microphone-Moving Matter of 1994."

"She was the drummer of the first band in the Elephant 6 collective, and a founding member of the collective," Robert reminds us again of a fact that can't be stated enough and should have been for decades.

"And she is a woman," Robert continues. "That last part shouldn't matter, but it does. It is a sad fact of rock history that women were not, except in scattered cases, viewed equally as musicians and producers until our generation. Hilarie was partly responsible for that."

In the summer of 2025, thirty years after the release of *Fun Trick Noisemaker*, Hilarie posted some photos of herself taken during downtime from an appearance by the High Water Marks at the Egersund Visefestival in Norway. In the photos, she is posing with paintings by her friend Steve Keene, the artist who painted the cover of the *Fun Trick Noisemaker* album.

One of the paintings is an interpretation by Steve of the cover of the Apples in Stereo album *The Discovery of a World Inside the Moone* from 2000.

Hilarie poses in 2025 with painter Steve Keene's take on the cover art of the Apples album The Discovery of a World Inside the Moone. *Photo by Per Ole Bratset.*

Seeing this photo reminds me of another comment Hilarie made during our conversations: "Make sure everyone knows your contributions."

If Robert needs to start taking more credit where credit is due, Hilarie needs to be given more credit where credit is overdue.

Robert and Hilarie's team vision for *Fun Trick Noisemaker* did not continue through subsequent Apples albums in the same way it did for other married couples in scene bands of the same era—Kim Gordon and Thurston Moore of Sonic Youth, Georgia Hubley and Ira Kaplan of Yo La Tengo, and Mimi Parker and Alan Sparhawk of Low, for example.

So, when I read, "The Apples are two distinct entities. There's the Apples with Hilarie and the Apples without Hilarie," which John Hill is quoted as saying in Adam Clair's *Endless Endless*, my now oft-admitted preconceived bias leads me to plug his words into my narrative as "Before: Good! After: Not good!"

Here are some combat metaphors!

I am required to let go of imagining Hilarie's opening drum salvo on "Tidal Wave" as the first shots fired in a war instead of a battle if I am going to hear *New Magnetic Wonder* and *Travellers in Space and Time* as their own works of art representing a new offensive by the Apples in Stereo, rather than what my bias tells me are hollow attempts at avoiding waving the white flag.

When I ask John to clarify his statement above, he says, "I'm proud to have been involved with those records."

I realize I am running out of time to revisit *New Magnetic Wonder* and *Travellers in Space and Time* with an open mind. The chapter is coming soon!

Robert reflects on Hilarie's artistic achievements thirty

years later with words that feel like he is being diplomatic but are also spoken in a genuine way that only a healed broken heart can say.

"I still want to support and honor Hilarie," Robert says. "She is a legendary drummer and songwriter as well as the mother of my child. She is sacred to me."

Twenty years earlier, it is hard to imagine how Robert managed to bring himself to support and honor Hilarie when he handled mixing 2004's *Songs About the Ocean*, the first album by the High Water Marks, the band Hilarie formed with Per Ole Bratset.

Hilarie and Per Ole first met at an Apples show in Oslo, Norway.

Robert says, "I did not blame her for leaving me for Per Ole. I gave them my blessings of goodwill. I mixed the first album by the High Water Marks during that period. Supporting Hilarie's path in music has been one of my primary goals since we started the collective."

Good for you, Robert. Damn, man. Personally, I would have lost my mind!

"We were both obsessed with a lot of the same bands," Hilarie says of meeting Per Ole. "Dinosaur Jr., Royal Trux, the Clean, Chrome, anything Flying Nun or Drag City, Pavement, Silver Jews, Black Flag, the Descendents, the Beatles, the Beach Boys . . . too many to name!

"He gave me a CD of his music, and it was exactly the thing I liked. The songwriting, guitar playing, everything. It seemed as though we were born to collaborate, so we started mailing tapes back and forth across the ocean.

"Eventually, I went back to Oslo and we almost finished *Songs About the Ocean* there. Instead, Per Ole moved to the US to finish the record in 2003, which by the end had been recorded across the ocean, in a hotel room, and at Pet Sounds."

Songs About the Ocean sounds like Hilarie stretching out, finally free of the constraints of a band dynamic—kind of like George Harrison unloading with *All Things Must Pass*—and now able to write songs with the confidence in knowing that she was in control of what would be completed, recorded, and released.

While Robert consoled himself at his console, his real reaction at the time could be heard on *010*, the debut album by Ulysses, the project mentioned previously that he formed in Lexington with John Ferguson, who would later join the Apples for *Travellers in Space and Time*.

010 is a breakup record by all accounts and includes song titles such as "Push You Away," "Change," and "Frustrated," all recorded and released in mono, as if to sonically represent the bleak occasion of being single.

These rock stars sure do live complicated lives!

010 was released concurrently with *Songs About the Ocean* on the same record label in 2004, just as Robert and Hilarie were in the midst of getting divorced.

"That turned out to be really lame for us because we were forever lumped in with Robert's side project instead of being a band of our own merit," Hilarie recalls.

To Hilarie's point, *Pitchfork* even reviewed the two records together, taking more of the same swipes at the Apples by bringing up the Cartoon Network *again*, but ultimately praising the "complex and considered arrangements" of the High Water Marks and the "sugar-coated melodies to spare" of the songs.

Hilarie was pregnant at the start of recording *New Magnetic Wonder*.

She says, "Per Ole and I had our son in 2005. Now, I was a mom of two kids, and I really wanted a break from touring. It was wearing me out. That whole life, the bickering with Robert, and how most of our friends picked a side and became his friends.

"I was piling up songs and being surrounded by a group of men for so many years, it made me question everything I'd known in my adult life and my perception of myself. I felt the loss of leaving the band before I left it."

Another husband-and-wife duo that presented a unified front until they didn't is Jack and Meg White of the White Stripes.

When I bring up how Hilarie's "flailing with intent" style preceded Meg's by more than a half decade, Hilarie reacts as if she has heard this before, and mentions that Jack and Meg attended a gig by the Apples at Zoot's Coffeehouse in Detroit prior to the release of the first single by the White Stripes in early 1998.

If some of Hilarie's playing really did rub off on Meg and Jack, I can't help but wonder what would have happened if some of Jack's relentless business ambitions had rubbed off on Hilarie and Robert. Part of Jack's immense tool chest of talents is shooting for the stars, and he has become one of the biggest because of it. This sort of ambition is rare, it isn't for everybody, and it is toxic for some.

What if deeper connections with their artistic brothers and sisters outside Elephant 6 during this era of the indie underground could have served to foster a shift in the artistic dynamic of the Apples? Could this have had an influence on how the band operated in their creative and business processes, and ultimately in how they were perceived and embraced by the public?

Without Meg, the White Stripes were no more.

On August 12, 2006, the Apples were on tour promoting the upcoming release of *New Magnetic Wonder*. It is impossible to overlook the location of the show that evening. At the close of the band's set in Athens, Georgia, the recognized home of Elephant 6, Hilarie announced she was quitting the Apples in Stereo.

"When our son was two, Per Ole and I started to record a follow-up to *Songs About the Ocean*," Hilarie says. "I recorded and mixed *Polar* [released in 2007] myself, and although not as many people heard it, I was really proud of my songwriting, engineering, and mixing on that record."

Unfortunately, with two young children, and a full-time job, Hilarie struggled to prioritize music at the time. In 2011, she and Per Ole began working on a third record that fell apart. Hilarie started feeling hopeless, and to pull herself out of it, she pivoted and preceded Robert's return to higher education by beginning to pursue a bachelor's degree while continuing to work full-time.

"There was not a lot of room for playing, though Per Ole and I continued to write songs, as always, and record them when we had time. Just the two of us, just like in the beginning," she remembers.

Soon, Hilarie received the Benjamin A. Gilman International Scholarship from the US Department of State, which would cover her tuition at the University of Oslo.

"The only way to accept the scholarship was to quit my job, and if I had to quit my job, I thought we might as well move back to Norway," she says. Hilarie and Per Ole had been living in Lexington for eleven years at this point. "We had been wanting to do it for so long, and I thought this might be the only chance."

Solar shimmer dancing on the street now
Swollen rivers collected at my feet now
I have seen the world this way
You can't give the clouds away
—"Can You" from *Ecstasy Rhymes* by the High Water Marks

Here are some weather metaphors!

In 2020, Norway's nature made the single from *Ecstasy Rhymes*—the first album by the High Water Marks in thirteen years—feel like wearing a light jacket on the first crisp day of fall.

Wow, you look sharp!

It took twenty-five years for the waters of "Tidal Wave" to resurface as the "swollen rivers" of "Can You," but when the skies cleared that morning, fans seeking Hilarie's unmistakable sunny sound basked in it again amid a forecast of much more new music to come.

Ecstasy Rhymes represents Hilarie's full-on return to the indie pop pantheon.

The false starts following *Songs About the Ocean* that were either overlooked or shelved as Hilarie split her focus with her new life, new family, and new country play as prologue when "Can You" spins. In fact, it is almost as if the Hilarie that left the Apples in 2006 had instantly traveled in space and time (so sorry!) to this watershed moment.

Ecstasy Rhymes sounds more like *Fun Trick Noisemaker* than *Travellers in Space and Time* sounds like the Apples in Stereo. The school of misogyny says, "Oh, Hilarie learned a lot from Robert starting with *Fun Trick Noisemaker*, and that's why *Ecstasy Rhymes* sounds this way." The school of feminism says, "Hilarie's contributions are a fundamental reason why *Fun Trick Noisemaker* sounds *that* way."

Hilarie's art has always been properly valid, but Hilarie's art has not always been properly valued.

She did not have the opportunity to fully express herself within the established confines of the group dynamic, and so it is revelatory that since recharging and reemerging in 2020, Hilarie has flexed and maintained a new standard.

The follow-up albums *Proclaimer of Things* in 2022, *Your Next Wolf* in 2023, a twentieth-anniversary edition of *Songs About the Ocean* in 2024 (featuring eight bonus tracks), and *Consult the Oracle* in 2025 continue to contribute to Hilarie's ongoing musical legacy.

The hopelessness that Hilarie was feeling in 2011 sounds like it is being addressed on *Consult the Oracle*'s title track fourteen years later:

Ask it a question, it tells you no lies
You'll see your future in somebody's eyes

Hmm: Robert told me to "ask," that is, "consult" Hilarie about the origin of the band's nicknames. He said Hilarie is "the oracle of good nicknames."

Trippy, man!

Hilarie's consistent musical output in the 2020s makes her the most prolific Elephant 6 artist at this time, a fact made even more notable because it is happening more than thirty years since she began releasing music.

Today, Hilarie's pop hooks are infused with lyrics informed by the decades of life she had yet to live when she contributed songs to the Apples in Stereo. Undercurrents of strife, and slight, threatening darkness are reflected in the illustrations that Per Ole provides for all the High Water Marks releases.

His work is completely different visually, but still brings Steve Keene to mind again anyway. Steve's *Fun Trick Noisemaker* cover art accurately reflected the Apples songs contained within. Per Ole's style similarly draws interest with a fun aesthetic until you realize you're looking at something a little more menacing than you initially thought.

The mutually shared songwriting real estate that was established in 2004 with *Songs About the Ocean* has continued through the current run of releases, which contain songs by Hilarie and songs by Per Ole.

"Per Ole and I decided from the outset that we were fifty-fifty, no matter what," Hilarie says about dealing with songwriting credits. She saw with her own eyes how a childhood friendship can be shaken by betrayal.

I mention to Hilarie that the four-way split "no matter what" philosophy has worked out well for R.E.M. (who would likely still be touring if not for Bill Berry's health issues) and U2 (who haven't had any public drama in nearly fifty years of existence).

It is a gift to the Elephant 6 community that Hilarie has the will to make so much music since returning to releasing records in 2020. She is giving new life to the distinct sound that she helped create as a founder of the Apples in Stereo, which is amazing considering that Robert's voice is not there.

Even without Robert's contributions, Hilarie's songs remind anyone who enjoys them to go back and also enjoy the Apples albums in which Hilarie's and Robert's voices sound like the shared air in which they were made, and sound like they were made for each other.

Hilarie says, "I am so lucky to have been a musician throughout my life."

Apple Picking, Pt. Nine
"I Want" from *Velocity of Sound*

"I Want" destroys!

As Robert and Hilarie drove away from Denver for the last time to continue their lives in Lexington, this two-minute bit of big audio dynamite could have been what was used to shake the building that housed the band's Pet Sounds studio to the ground.

The atypical, unexpected chord, followed by a simple one-two-three fill on the snare and tom that goes before the start of each verse, feels like a downer, and I don't mean vibe, I mean Vicodin. This is concentrated drama, and it is potent.

Robert couldn't produce the Ramones, but he could approximate the metaphorical raw power of their production and mix it with the literal *Raw Power* of an unhinged Stooges.

Perfectly contrasting this unnerving presentation is Hilarie's vocal delivery. Relaxed, poised, and cool, she knows exactly how to place herself against what feels like a Marshall stack pushed up against your skull, or maybe a face full of Jeff Price's blown-out car speakers, even through cheap earbuds.

Then there is her drumming, of course. The way Hilarie hits the snare drum is a bad, bad mood. Considerate listeners can draw the connection between the person singing and the person snaring.

The louder, the better. Even ear doctors agree.

•

When I ask Robert for three "Apple Picking" picks, he responds right away with two of Hilarie's songs. Then, he quickly added "Tidal Wave" and "Energy." I immediately called him out for flubbing the assignment—a mathematician should know that three songs is not four songs!

Ten minutes later, I receive a frantic-feeling text from Robert saying he would like to change his choices, completely negating my original premise, but validating another at the same time. The reason I wanted to know what everyone would say without thinking was because I wanted to psychoanalyze their responses in the context of the band's entire catalog.

"I will do another nonthinking response," Robert wrote back, to which I replied, "Thanks, but no. I am publishing all of this!" Robert went on to complete a third flub, by replying with a fifth song, the Hilarie track "Questions and Answers" from what Robert referred to in the text as "our psych EP."

Fans love when artists mention a fundamental work— in this case, the extraordinary Apples in Stereo EP *Her Wallpaper Reverie* from 1999—in such a matter-of-fact way, and I am one of them.

"'Q&A' is amazing," Robert said. It is also amazing, in terms of my psychoanalysis, that out of the five songs Robert mentioned, three of them are Hilarie's.

Apple Picking, Pt. Ten
"Questions and Answers" from *Her Wallpaper Reverie*
Hilarie's unending cool is epitomized in her compact drum

fills. She doesn't need to show you more than that. She shows exactly what she decides you need to see.

Robert concurs: "She avoids drum fills and fancy hi-hat flourishes except for when absolutely necessary."

"Questions and Answers" is another example, like "Tidal Wave," of a killer Hilarie drum intro, except this time she lays waste in two seconds flat.

In the song's first verse, Hilarie unexpectedly drops her vocal register at the end of the line, "Just ask a question that will make it go away," setting up for an undeniable and memorable chorus melody that provides the brightest bit of balance on *Her Wallpaper Reverie*, the band's darkest collection of tunes sonically and, in many ways, thematically.

> *They're sending me a picture of the moon*
> *and star-mapped skies for travelers in tune*
> —"Questions and Answers"

A George Harrison–style solo sends us back into the indelible chorus again, punctuated by tambourine work that is varied and complimentary, rather than simply adding another inserted percussion element. How often is tambourine work deserving of mention?

It is a rare discussion that involves continually referring back to a songwriter's drumming when discussing their songs, but similar to Robert's writing, in which he considers the eventual production during his composition process, Hilarie seems to do the same when writing songs that she knows she will play drums on.

Robert says, "She is as loud as John Bonham, but grooves like Buddy Miles. She pounds like Pavement and blares like the Ramones."

Not enough songs fade to a close anymore like "Questions and Answers" does. It is a fascinating conceit to feel as if, even when we leave, the music never stops. With that, we have this book's second reference to one Grateful Dead song.

Apple Picking, Pt. Eleven
"Strawberryfire" from *Her Wallpaper Reverie*

It has been a couple of pages since a Robert Schneider flub.

"I'm also putting 'Strawberryfire' as an alternate," Robert says, ignoring my instructions once again. This makes four flubs!

Robert suggested a total of six songs after my initial, quite specific, request for three. He then asked if he could rethink his choices entirely after my initial, quite specific, request to only name songs that immediately came to mind. I am pointing this out now to account, not to reprimand.

Honestly, I am actually thrilled that Robert brought up "Strawberryfire."

I have been thinking about Hilarie's drum fills for years prior to writing about them here. In late 2024, I published a Substack article titled "Can AI-Generated Music Have a Soul? Does the Best Drum Fill of All-Time Prove That the Answer Is No?" This piece was inspired by conversations with Robert about his ongoing experimental music path, which includes composing using generative AI as a companion. In it, I claim that music made this way can never, and will never, contain the soul of music made by humans.

In the story, Robert and I chat about how the vocals on the songs he generates sound eerily like Robert, but at the same time not, which is likely due to the AI model that he uses being taught by his distinctive voice, which occurs so frequently due to his large catalog of recordings. Combine this fact with Robert's advanced ability at constructing and tweaking prompts destined to access that information, and the rendered results are haunting.

I state in the piece, "Since we're speaking about the Apples in Stereo in the data set, I want to use some of Robert's organically own music to prove my point about the inability of the rabbit hole of the soul to go deep with AI."

I then go on to offer up what I call "the best drum fill of all-time" as proof. That fill is played by Hilarie on the song "Strawberryfire."

I continue in the piece, "One listen to 'Strawberryfire,' and you will not only hear the influences that you are meant to hear—the elements that AI might learn from—but you will also hear a vocal from Robert that is deeply rich in psychedelic detachment while being completely moored in emotion at the same time. It is human."

I continue, "Then, at 2:36, is a moment that has stuck with me through the 25 years since this record was released. This moment is my smoking gun. Hilarie executes a fill that is so perfectly restrained and compact in its touch that it feels like a balm—like a hand on my shoulder."

As I continue with my minutiae, I start to understand why a producer and percussionist would argue over a thirty-year-old crash cymbal recording.

"That is a choice that only a human mind and heart working in tandem can create in a moment of psychological and biological magic. It is human. It is a head-shaking flex," I rant at Robert. "I am unconvinced AI would ever make this musical choice no matter how many forests were decimated to power the renderings to get there!"

"I am so honored that you like the drum fill on that," Hilarie says when I ask her to comment on the drum fill I gave my "best drum fill of all-time" award to, which obviously means I love it, not "like" it, c'mon!

Hilarie continues, "What excites me most is the way Robert miked the drums up, and then added this super-psychedelic delay that is reminiscent of 'Strawberry Fields Forever,' also a song filled with incredible drum fills."

Okay, *now* Hilarie acknowledges her "Strawberryfire" fill is incredible. Thank you. I feel seen.

Confirming what Robert said earlier, Hilarie explains, "I try to use drum fills very sparingly, but when I do, I try to make it subtle. I went for something laid-back, tasteful, but robust at the same time on 'Strawberryfire.'"

"Strawberryfire" is my favorite song by the Apples in Stereo. It gives off the same unease I feel when listening to "I Am the Walrus," and combines that with the acid-laced nostalgic majesty of the aforementioned "Strawberry Fields Forever." It is a masterful combination of the creepy candor and self-possessed production of both.

I am not alone in loving this song. "Strawberryfire" is one of the most popular tracks by the Apples in Stereo, with three million plays on Spotify alone, proving that listeners have a taste for tunes with "Strawberry" in the title, and also for having their minds messed with.

As it turns out, my use of "Strawberryfire" to prove to Robert that AI is soulless has an underpinning of irony.

"'Strawberryfire' was the first Apples song to use a computer in a central way," Robert tells me. "I based the song around a loop I built on a computer, and then we bounced between the tape machine and the computer to produce psychedelic effects."

After Hilarie left the Apples, new drummer John Dufilho rightly continued to faithfully perform her fill with the too-cool touch it deserves. That's how the song goes, after all.

In my early teens, seeing Sheila E. handle her business behind the kit for Prince was my frame of reference for how a woman powers a group mostly made of men. She is rightly showcased as such in the 1987 concert film that shares its title with the classic album *Sign o' the Times*.

In my early twenties, I discovered Sheila's opposite in terms of flash, but she was no less foundational. Moe Tucker was not supposed to be the permanent drummer for the Velvet Underground. She was only supposed to sit in for one show, but it only took the one show to know that the one was Moe.

Meg White wouldn't come along for a couple more years, and while I adore the Go-Go's and the Janet Weiss–era Sleater-Kinney, neither had to put up with a bunch of dudes to get the job done.

I have always been fascinated by the dynamic of female drummers in otherwise male-dominated bands.

A few weeks after first noticing the Apples in Stereo and the intriguing *Science Faire* compilation cover art with its mysterious "Projects by THE APPLES in stereo" designation, I got my first look at, and listen to, the band. This was 1996. It took a minute to find out, but when I did, Hilarie became the new Moe to me.

Hilarie hit hard while presenting as light. Her deceptively simple style—like Meg's later—was a way of performing that is so straightforward, it becomes key to the band's sonic integrity, kind of like a recipe with so few ingredients that it only works if those ingredients are top-notch. Cut corners and you've got a flop on your hands.

Apple Picking, Pts. Twelve & Thirteen
"20 Cases Suggestive Of . . ." from *The Discovery of a World Inside the Moone* & "Winter Must Be Cold" from *Fun Trick Noisemaker*

"I love all of Hilarie's songs," Eric says, "but '20 Cases Suggestive Of . . .' and 'Winter Must Be Cold' are what pop into my head. On both of those songs, her voice is so cool and beautiful, but the music under it has an insistence, drive, and purpose. They sound different from other Apples songs, but obviously are Apples songs."

"It's based on a book about reincarnation," Hilarie explains. "It's a scientific investigation of cases of reincarnation in India, specifically cases about children who recall details of another life. It left an impression on me."

In addition to drums, Hilarie plays the cool tremolo guitars on this recording.

"I had written the chords and the melody to the song already, and the lyrics came quickly after reading the book," she says.

"I love hearing Robert on Hilarie's songs too," Eric continues. "He sings and plays in a way that he doesn't on his own songs."

"Winter Must Be Cold" was also picked by Robert.

This early *Fun Trick Noisemaker* recording features a rollicking country-dirt-road guitar figure underneath Hilarie's shy yet sly vocal. It is noticeable when returning to the band's earliest material how tentative they were at the start compared to the rapid rate of their growth.

Hilarie's vocal confidence develops immeasurably throughout the years, but it is notable that her early delivery works for this song anyway. The Apples always made the best of their limitations—and even let those limitations inspire ingenuity—instead of being constricted by them.

It is also apparent that from the very beginning Robert's and Hilarie's voices together on tape is a special sound. Divorce is common, but the divorce of common voices shouldn't be.

The subject matter of the next chapter, and subsequently its title, was already set months before I said, "Wow!" out loud when I looked at the lyrics for "Winter Must Be Cold," saw the "ring" line that literally alludes to where we are going next, and heard Robert singing it along with Hilarie on the recording.

Winter must be cold because
You already missed the spring
I won't give it up until I get my ring
—"Winter Must Be Cold"

There are no coincidences.

8. GRABBING AT THE RING: "PEPSI WAS OUR CHOICE, PHOTOS WERE NOT!"

Warning: This chapter discusses the music industry. If you are sensitive to reading about corrupt institutions, please skip ahead!

Avoiding money and fame while not avoiding money and fame is tricky business.

Before we go any further, I owe you an apology. I didn't remember that I had already titled this chapter when I had promised earlier to not make any more *Lord of the Rings* puns. "Grabbing at the ring," as I first mentioned in chapter 1, is a phrase that I used in my conversations with Robert about the phase of the band's career leading up to and after Hilarie's announcement that she was leaving the group.

It is a phrase I have used often during my career in the music industry. It is the moment when a band that has built a fundamental part of its marketability on not marketing itself at all reaches a point of wanting to, and sometimes needing to, reach a larger audience to stay artistically relevant and financially solvent.

"Grabbing at the ring" is when opportunities for money, fame, and validation are so great that they become irresistible, even for the most grounded and supported person. The consequences can be disastrous for the artist on a personal level, and often, the consequences can be disastrous for the art as well.

It is a challenging moment to navigate and, while noting Robert's claim that I am mistaken about "the ring," and with respect to his perspective, this is what I saw happening with the Apples during the album cycles for *New Magnetic Wonder* and *Travellers in Time and Space*.

As stated, "grabbing at the ring" is mostly about marketing, not art, at least at first, which is why I agreed to "wonder" about *New Magnetic Wonder* and *Travellers in Space and Time* with an open mind, something I did not have about those albums when they were released. I had previously judged these records based on my preconceived bias about what I was seeing instead of what I could be hearing. This is a typical type of treatment for a band facing this moment in their career, and I admittedly treated it typically.

Sometimes the art can be confused with the marketing of the art. The condemned building on Elati Street in Denver is "authentic." The *American Idol* advertorial is "not authentic." By the way, this is the second time I have ever typed the word "advertorial" in my entire life.

As contemplated a few pages back, the Apples with Hilarie is "good," and the Apples without Hilarie is "not good." These perspectives are without nuance at least and, at worst, completely disregard the art itself, which will always be fixed in time.

The music industry is highly skilled at ruining the mystery of artistry. Once you are aware of the machine, it is difficult to be excited by what appears to be careerism unrelated to the art, such as a song showing up on *American*

Idol, as "Energy" did. Don't get me wrong, the opportunity and exposure are infinitely beneficial if leveraged to generate quick income and quick notoriety for the organization, but quick income and quick notoriety ignores the art.

In the specific case of the Apples in Stereo, a mom being proud of her son's song on *American Idol* has a value that can't be measured, but this son's songs tend to be very sad, and no amount of positioning them in the realm of pop culture changes that. Some sad songs feel even more sad because of how upbeat they are, as if the positivity is working overtime to mask the sadness.

The Elephant 6 core lore depicts the collective as a bunch of iconoclastic rebels reluctant to claim fame, or to even claim infamy, amid artistic ethics and personal morality tied to shunning the spotlight. Maybe it was because the mile-high atmosphere put their heads closer to the clouds but, as you have read, the Apples flirted with the bigger music business, and the business of bigger fame, from the beginning.

It is ironic that it took the efforts and work of the entire collective to make the Elephant 6 myth valuable, but when Robert tried to give it back to them, they didn't want it. As we will see, yet another talent of Robert's—for better, worse, or indifferent—was in finding funding for his "Projects by THE APPLES in stereo."

"The main thing is, I wasn't trying to make a living," Robert says. "I was trying to gain funding for a project and live on a shoestring. They funded all of my ambitions, and all of my friends' ambitions," he reveals, regarding the lucrative sync deals he struck.

While arguments will be made as to what was

compromised and what wasn't, Robert is resolute: "I gave up nothing."

Self-made artists of this era were petrified of being perceived as "selling out," while at the same time wanting the notoriety, the accolades, and the ability to get their work in front of as many people as possible. Unfortunately, too few realized that to "sell out without selling out" simply required understanding that it is possible to work the system from within.

Signing a record deal is an exciting time for most bands. The Apples started their career already "signed" to the Elephant 6 Recording Co. They did not have to experience what unfortunately befalls many bands the day after they snap a picture of themselves gathered around a boardroom table while holding up a contract with the ink still wet.

For too many hardworking musicians, the reality of that day—no matter how cool, supportive, and encouraging a label staff may be—is that the corporation behind those cool people is now going to put money into you and your creativity, and therefore expects something of you that wasn't expected when you were making the music just for fun. These expectations can serve to distract, add pressure, and ultimately alter the creation of the work itself.

For some, that is.

"The Apples used the music industry as nothing more than a sandbox," Robert says. "I have been focused my entire life on avoiding money, avoiding fame, and avoiding attention." Even though Robert has been shy to claim artistic credit that he is clearly owed, when it comes to doing business, the Apples have always been in the "sandbox."

Soon, Robert would have enough sand to build a castle. Shout-out to Jimi Hendrix!

"When we put out that seven-inch, we had so many people call us," Hilarie says in *Endless Endless*, going on to mention "a call from Warner Bros." and "being taken out to nice dinners." Her comments proved prophetic when Warner Bros. subsidiary Sire Records picked up the band's second album, *Tone Soul Evolution*, for release in 1997.

Signing with a major label subsidiary in 1997 predates my preconceived bias about Robert's flirtation with the seduction of "selling out" by nearly a decade. The deal done with the legendary label run by the legendary mogul Seymour Stein was sealed over one of those "nice dinners."

Robert says, "Seymour signed us himself! He came to see us play in Philadelphia at Upstairs at Nick's. He was super cool, and we went to an Italian restaurant after. Every major label tried to sign us at the time, but, obviously, Seymour was special."

I asked Robert what he ordered that night. "I'm pretty sure it was spaghetti, garlic bread, and salad," he says.

I submitted a request with the restaurant to verify Robert's order, hoping to hear back by press time. I believe Robert when he says he ate spaghetti, but I have yet to substantiate this. Sorry.

Robert's claim of avoiding money and fame seems sincere and is in line with the ideals of his collective, but once you're inside the system, objectivity and sincerity are scarce. His altruism may have guided his actions, but the nefarious nature of the music industry tends to separate artists from their artistic ideology.

Still, Robert *is* the "glossies in the garbage" guy. He *is* okay with being perceived as a dick. He is the guy who got dumped and then mixed the album his ex-wife made with her new partner, which would have caused some people (me!) to have a nervous breakdown.

"See? Fame and money do not always mean a shallow person," Robert says. "The way I see it, if one engages in games with well-defined rules, then one should play well, compete well, and feel proud of achievements."

"An economy is such a game," he continues. "I have pretty good thoughts about money. Money is converting energy from one form into another." Robert's philosophy about money is sound, but a sound philosophy does not guarantee that money won't fundamentally alter the sound.

Robert says, "I am afraid of accumulating money, which helps to keep my anxiety level down," but I am afraid that Robert's accumulation of money will keep his artistic level down.

Artists must be willing to walk into the music business with the intent to alter it, and the resolve to not let it alter them or their art. Otherwise, artists are at its mercy.

I want to believe in *New Magnetic Wonder* and *Travellers in Space and Time* as works of art defining a new phase of the Apples in Stereo and not evidence of the band's waning creativity.

Let's see what happens.

Avoiding money is easy when there is no money to avoid.

Tone Soul Evolution—the band's 1997 sophomore album that Seymour Stein signed over spaghetti (meal unsubstantiated!) to release on Sire Records—marked the first time that the Apples in Stereo were recording in a "real" studio, and Robert took advantage of the opportunity to learn everything he could.

"If it weren't for Michael Deming [at Studio .45], I

wouldn't have learned how to use a studio," Robert says.

Robert told *Tape Op*, "He taught me how to use a patch bay. He taught me how to use a tape machine with more than eight tracks. He taught me how to use a compressor. It was incredible."

Robert pictured during the recording of Tone Soul Evolution. *"This is in the studio B room at Studio .45 in Hartford," John Hill says. "That's John's guitar," Robert elaborates. "I played it while we adjusted John's amps." The milk crate pictured on the right is also noteworthy. It sold in an Elephant 6 memorabilia auction for just shy of $2.8 million. (Correction: Robert says, "Untrue. I keep my synthesizer supplies in that crate now.") Photo by John Hill, courtesy of the Apples in Stereo.*

"He was a great collaborator," Robert adds, "although I did butt horns with him."

Robert wasn't the only member of the Apples who had difficulties during these sessions.

"It's the only record that we recorded at a studio like that," Hilarie told *Fifteen Questions*. "We lived in the studio, which was in Hartford, Connecticut. The surrounding area was kind of depressing. I had a lot of anxiety caused by the engineer who exuded negativity, and the long days could be brutal."

When the sessions were completed, Robert took the mixes of *Tone Soul Evolution* to his mastering engineer of choice. Michael was not pleased with the results, and told Robert so.

"We were super happy," Robert remembers. "But when Mike heard it, he flipped out because we had compressed his hi-fi recording. He asked to remaster it, and it probably did sound better in a technical sense, but it never kicked the way the original master did."

The version of the master that Michael delivered is the version of *Tone Soul Evolution* that was ultimately released. The word of the day, "furious," came up again at the time— let's just put it that way.

"In the end, I trusted Mike, and always regretted it," Robert says. "I was never happy with the album because the master sounded too fluffy and soft."

This wrong was recently made right. "When we reissued *Tone Soul Evolution* a few years ago, we used the original master," Robert notes.

Several years after those fraught sessions, the band received word that a major telecommunications company was interested in licensing the *Tone Soul Evolution* track "Shine a Light," a deal that was potentially worth nearly $1 million to be split among all the interested parties.

As it goes with these kinds of advertising opportunities, a decision had to be made immediately, and the client required access to an instrumental mix of the song, also immediately.

Luckily, but not without much distress, the lingering difficulties of the *Tone Soul Evolution* sessions did not get in the way of securing a quick and acceptable "Shine a Light" instrumental mix, and the deal got done.

Unfortunately, as it goes in the business of show, some organizations that were supposed to be on the band's side chose to leverage the band's urgency to close the deal against them by claiming more of the licensing fee for themselves, ruining relationships in the process.

Still, that process continued.

In 2001, *The New York Times Magazine* published a piece about the Apples in Stereo titled "For Rock Bands, Selling Out Isn't What It Used to Be," which focused on a deal the band did for the use of "Strawberryfire" from "our psych EP" in a Sony commercial.

The logic that Robert uses to justify taking money from giant corporations sounds twisted in the mind of a skeptical, sometimes cynical, eyebrow-raising dude like me, but in light of Robert's explanation, it starts to make some sense, although it could sound to some (like me!) as merely a justification.

Robert insists, "Not selling out is very important to me. For me, 'selling out' means paying lip service to the music industry and playing their game, and 'not selling out' means finding my own way to achieve the goals for our band and collective."

It seems wild to say that not having to kiss up to an indie or even the subsidiary of a major record label justifies taking giant checks from multinational monolithic corporations. If I have to, here's how I would twist that logic in order to be okay with all the extra zeros:

Faceless corporations that nakedly offer cash for art do so in a quick and quite literally immediate transaction, as we saw with the band's deal for "Shine a Light" described above.

The music industry, however, draws out a relationship predicated on "teamwork," and based on "artwork," in which the team often seeks to undermine the band's earnings while meddling with their creative process and completed work.

Robert sums it similarly when I pointedly ask, "How do you go from being the guy who rips up press photos on principle to licensing your flagship song 'Energy' to Pepsi?"

"Pepsi was our choice, photos were not!" he answers.

"SpinART disregarded our choice and printed the photo *they* liked. That went against our own control of our own band, so I established early on that that was not going to work."

Robert points out additional ways that the band literally did not put their money where their mouth is.

"As vegetarians, we would not license our songs to restaurants that sold meat," he says. "Also, unlike many bands, we would not license our songs to the alcohol industry, and we refused to have alcohol banners behind us onstage."

In this latter case, Robert had the band's audience in mind as well.

"Alcohol is bad, and many of our listeners were young people. Alcohol is responsible for the abuse of women, and many of our listeners are women."

This idea about being conscious of abuse goes even further.

"As pacifists, we would not license our songs to the military," Robert explains. "We turned down lots of corporations that we thought of as evil."

When it came to other types of corporate behemoths, however, Robert reasons, "We turned down many large offers because we had full creative control contractually, and we claimed it at every turn. I saw Samsung, Pepsi, Sony, and other ads like that as radio play—this is our song being broadcast to every household by an alternative means."

Avoiding fame is easy when there is no fame to avoid.

We have arrived at the moment in every rock 'n' roll band's history when Elijah Wood enters the picture.

Elijah Wood and Robert Schneider captured in a candid moment discussing the benefits of being photographed barefoot with your friend. Elijah released the last two Apples albums on his Simian Records label. Photo by Joshua Kessler.

The *Lord of the Rings* actor was responsible for coming up with the "bustle in your hedgerow" lyric on Led Zeppelin's "Stairway to Heaven." (This claim has been debunked.

"Stairway to Heaven" was written ten years prior to Elijah's birth.)

Now Elijah would change the course of the Apples in Stereo story.

Elijah first saw the Apples perform in 2001 at the yearly South by Southwest music festival in Austin, Texas. He approached the band at the show, became fast friends with Robert, and kept in touch. Four years later, when the band's contract with SpinART expired, Elijah negotiated a deal to release *New Magnetic Wonder*.

Remember, Robert was aware of avoiding money and fame, but money and fame were not aware of avoiding Robert. He could have taken much more, and was conscious of turning away opportunities, but his subconscious had other ideas.

"I had quite a lot of money from the licenses," he says, "So I had the opportunity to fund *New Magnetic Wonder* independently. It felt good to be free."

It had already been several years since the release of *Velocity of Sound* in 2002, and Robert was enjoying spending as much time and money as he wanted to make *New Magnetic Wonder*.

"We decided we wanted to go with Elijah before the record was done. He didn't seem to have a working label yet, but at the time it didn't matter, because we didn't have a record yet.

"That Elijah is a famous movie star was random and totally unrelated," Robert says, as if to acknowledge my consistently expressed skepticism. "I make friends with people, and I involve them as friends," Robert explains.

Still, Elijah's fame would be a boon to the band's visibility. The back-end resources provided by the partnership of

Simian Records—the label Elijah eventually founded with the distribution and marketing infrastructure of Yep Roc Records—made this deal play perfectly on paper.

Would it play perfectly on double vinyl and compact disc too? I guess Elijah didn't see the return on investment potential of a *New Magnetic Wonder* cassette. I get that.

Skeptical, sometimes cynical, eyebrow-raising dudes—of which I am one as previously stated—could perceive offering up your band as the test case for a record label controlled by a celebrity as a risky move.

Robert had already experienced how fast fortune warped the future of lifelong friendships. This time, would a fast friendship warp the future of Robert's artistic fortune?

Back in 2006, Robert had already shown the disinterest in fame that undermined the more shameless aspects of self-promotion and need for attention that, even if you are an artist who claims to not want or care about one, are required to create a lasting legacy.

Robert may not have cared about money, but now he had it anyway. Robert may not have cared about fame, but now he could have it anyway. Robert may not have cared to be at personal and professional crossroads, but he arrived there anyway.

Avoiding the inevitable is easy when there is no inevitable to avoid.

"I don't remember why Robert's nickname was 'the Jet,'" Hilarie says.

Robert does.

"'The Jet' is because I am always the last person to come out of anywhere. Like, the hotel, the gas station . . ."

Or the fog of your drummer quitting the band just ahead of the release of the highest-stakes album of your career?

It is intentional that the "classic" configuration of the Apples in Stereo from 2005—Fuzz, the Jet, Hilarie (nickname still unknown), and PRE—is pictured on the cover of this book, close to the somber time of their split, instead of ten years earlier in 1995, close to the optimistic time of their first hit.

During this shoot, the Apples in Stereo didn't know they were being photographed for the cover of a book titled The Apples in Stereo. *No one in the band seems to know the identity of the mystery photographer seen in the reflection of Robert's sunglasses either. (L–R): John Hill, Robert Schneider, Hilarie Sidney, Eric Allen. Courtesy of the Apples in Stereo.*

"We were so young in our thirties!" Hilarie jokes when I contact her about this photo. No one in the band knows who took it.

Robert responds, "You can see the photographer in the sunglasses."

Yeah. Thanks, dude.

In 1995, when the members of the Apples were in their early twenties, there was promise everywhere they looked.

No mistakes made. No limits. No mortality. If this sounds familiar, and you aren't in a rock band, then you realize that we all feel this way at this age. Some of us look back and wonder how we are still alive. Some of us look back and remember some who aren't alive. Some of us aren't able to look back at all.

The Apples as pictured in 2005 are the "all three" Apples: the band is now a decade past proving their prowess at perfect "pop."

They have masterfully contrasted that skill with their most "art" impulses on "our psych EP"—1999's *Her Wallpaper Reverie*—the most diverse of the band's work that, even as a truncated album, contains two of their most-streamed songs.

I am using "our psych EP" as much as possible—it's so good.

The emotionally "deep" songwriting from Robert, Hilarie, and now Eric, if under-recognized, has been further vouched for by the universal acclaim for Robert's artistic achievements as producer and collaborator on *In the Aeroplane Over the Sea*, which, by even 2005, had already become widely regarded as the classic Robert predicted it would be.

Hilarie is so right!

Looking back from our forties and fifties, we really were "so young in our thirties." It is a part of life that seems like it can only be understood with perspective, as if it is a lost age during the time it is being lived.

Tempting fate throughout our twenties has armed us

with practical knowledge that we can use to try again, to try better, to try harder. Now, we have the experience that leads us to believe that even if we come up short this time, the attempt was all our own, made with an ability laborious to learn and an acumen elusive but earned.

Our thirties are actually when we become serious for the first time. We have had a taste of success at what we set out to do for fun, and it *was* fun, until it started to look like the freedom of fun would become the commitment of forever. We start to realize that life may be shorter than it is long.

Fierce independence can get in the way of personal growth, especially when you get past the idealism of your twenties and have boxed yourself in as idealistic above all else. You love the security of the box. You want to break out of the box. You don't know who you are without the box.

Robert and Hilarie were already divorced with a young child when the photo on the previous page was taken. It represents artists whose lives are in transition. Hilarie looks fierce, determined, and independent. She would be out of the band a year later.

Robert looks acute, aloof, and alone. He is now a serious thirtysomething and would have to act like a serious thirtysomething to bring about the latest version of the Apples in Stereo minus Hilarie.

Robert still had too much to do!

He could not afford to be "the Jet" anymore. Robert could, however, afford to pay for the production of *New Magnetic Wonder* on his own. Perhaps more importantly for Robert's well-being, he was also able to use these funds to support the band on the road.

Self-preservation certainly plays a part in leading Robert to officially bring Bill Doss of the Olivia Tremor Control into the Apples in Stereo following Hilarie's departure.

Bill was already involved in making *New Magnetic Wonder*. Robert had brought many other friends into the production process as well, but having his childhood best friend with him on the road could bring comfort from someone close who knew Robert to his core.

This idea is lent even more substance in the sad light of hindsight. Bill's passing in 2012 motivated Robert to disprove the slow speed of "the Jet," when he moved immediately into his current math career faster than any ad agency could cut a sync deal.

It was as if Robert escaped into mathematics because music betrayed him. Friends dying. Friendships dying. It was as if to say, "I can't put myself in harm's way anymore."

The amount of personal loss that Robert has suffered is noteworthy. It is astounding that he has lost so many of the closest allies and advocates who emboldened and encouraged his belief in his artistic vision.

Robert reiterates his ideological claims once again, but with a shattering addition this time.

Unlike the previous explanations and clarifications that Robert offered to justify his proximity to money and fame throughout his career, his current justification of why it only mattered as a means to an end is the most convincing of all.

"I don't care about money. I avoid fame. My best friend passed away."

Whether Robert grabbed at the ring doesn't matter if it brings you closer to the music that is fixed in perpetuity. That is all that matters. Let's see!

Back in chapter 1, Robert said, "*New Magnetic Wonder*

achieves the vision of *Fun Trick Noisemaker*," the debut album by the Apples in Stereo, which Robert says was "*our* album," referring to his twin vision with Hilarie.

When *Fun Trick Noisemaker* was made, all that the Apples had was the freedom of youth and the freedom of vision. Now, with money, Robert could buy back the autonomy that was no longer a given. Robert was free and without any artistic impediments or obligations to anyone but himself.

"No strife on that album!" Robert exclaims about *New Magnetic Wonder.*

I comment that "strife is part of what makes the records slap," and Robert responds, "If you believe that, then *New Magnetic Wonder* is your favorite Apples album! It embodies our greatest ambition, our greatest collection of songs, and also our greatest period of strife that ended with our band almost breaking up at the end."

The "no strife" and "greatest period of strife" contradiction aside, I asked Robert for a sales pitch and he is giving me one. I realize now that I have been letting Hilarie's comment about being "left out of a lot of what happened" on *New Magnetic Wonder* keep me from the other side of that coin, which is that, if she was "left out a lot," then she was also included in a lot.

Robert repeats, "*New Magnetic Wonder* is *Fun Trick Noisemaker* perfected, and Hilarie was a big part of it. We were a full band at that time, not realizing the end was near for her involvement."

Then Hilarie adds, "There are a couple of great songs. I love my drums on 'Skyway.' I like 'Play Tough,' '7 Stars,' and 'Beautiful Machine,' I think it's called?"

Just like when Robert says, "our psych EP," I love the lore that is evoked when artists don't remember the names of their own songs. We will discuss "Beautiful Machine" (which is not exactly what it's called) in the next chapter.

New Magnetic Wonder follows Robert's divorce from Hilarie, and *Travellers in Space and Time* follows Hilarie's divorce from the band.

Only now am I thinking of the possibility that these records represent artistic freedom for Robert—or at least freedom from ten years of his previous perspective—that he couldn't have had before making them.

9. WHAT'S IT GOING TO TAKE TO GET YOU INTO *NEW MAGNETIC WONDER* TODAY?

It is confusing to be both the audience and the author.

I have been dismissive of the final two records by the Apples in Stereo because of personal issues with the change in personnel. I admit that Hilarie leaving the Apples on the eve of the release of *New Magnetic Wonder* poisoned the album for me.

Is my preconceived bias keeping me from songs that could make a difference in my life?

I attempted to explore these questions with my therapist.

He said, "I have no idea what you are talking about, Josh!" So I called up the Italian restaurant where Seymour Stein signed the Apples in Stereo to Sire Records and asked the owner. She hung up on me, but not before confirming Robert's spaghetti order from that night, so I call it a soft success.

The above never happened, but this does:

I snap-judge art without thinking. My gut speaks for my heart and mind when it comes to the story I tell myself with my eyes and ears. The intent of this book is to bring you closer to the songs of the Apples in Stereo. In writing it, I accepted that my preconceived bias about the band's final two records would be challenged.

●

Hilarie left the band so close to the release date of *New Magnetic Wonder* that we see new drummer John Dufilho performing to Hilarie's track in the music video for the album's first single "Energy." It is an unexpectedly poignant reminder that Hilarie was not around to revel in the biggest song she ever performed on by the band she was a founding member of.

Because *New Magnetic Wonder* was released amid the departure of one of the band's founders, I became disinterested in the Apples at the time. I felt the same way about R.E.M. when Michael Stipe, Mike Mills, and Peter Buck continued making records as a trio after drummer Bill Berry amicably left the band in 1997 due to health reasons.

Still, unlike the Bill Berry–less R.E.M. records I haven't heard, Hilarie is behind the drums throughout *New Magnetic Wonder*, save for her two tracks, "Sunndal Song" and "Sunday Sounds."

"He played drums on both of Hilarie's songs," Robert confirms when I ask about how it seems to have slipped under the radar that Jeff Mangum of Neutral Milk Hotel appears on *New Magnetic Wonder* playing drums on the songs where Hilarie takes over on vocals and guitar.

It is odd to me that this factoid is not more well-known considering the hunger among Jeff's fans to collect and catalog information about his whereabouts and activities.

"We just didn't make a big deal about it," Robert concludes. This reminds me of Derek Smalls telling his manager Ian Faith, in our second reference to *This Is Spinal Tap* that "Making a big thing out of it would have been a good idea," although comparing Jeff to Stonehenge is a quick escalation to eleven.

In reality, it is difficult to imagine compartmentalizing the work to be done at a recording session—or how the session even came together—considering the lingering feelings regarding Robert's contributions to Neutral Milk Hotel not being properly acknowledged.

(L–R): Hilarie Sidney, Jeff Mangum, Robert Schneider. Jeff played bass in an early version of the Apples and sometimes traded roles with Hilarie onstage. The two of them did it again over twenty years later when Jeff backed Hilarie on her two tunes from the penultimate Apples album New Magnetic Wonder. *Photo by Lisa Janssen, courtesy of the Apples in Stereo.*

Remember, in the couple of years prior to beginning the sessions for *New Magnetic Wonder*, Robert and Hilarie are breaking up; Robert is mixing a record by the High Water Marks, the new band that Hilarie and her now-husband Per Ole Bratset have formed; and, not long after that, Hilarie is happy, pregnant, and contemplating leaving the band.

During all of this, Robert has aligned himself professionally with Elijah Wood, one of the most visible movie stars in the world on the heels of his starring role in *The Lord of the Rings* films that have grossed in excess of $3 billion worldwide.

Either the emotional maturity of these people is staggering, they are very good at ignoring their feelings, or all this mess can be heard in the work. The latter is the best-case scenario for the listener.

The Apples records that move me so much are the ones where Hilarie is fully present and invested in the band's future. I am sensitive in my exchanges with Robert when it comes to directly tying my thoughts about the artistic value of *New Magnetic Wonder* and *Travellers in Space and Time* to Hilarie's imminent departure, and then absence, from the Apples.

Luckily, as mentioned earlier, Robert had his best friend and lifelong collaborator Bill Doss of the Olivia Tremor Control close by to soften the situation. Just like John Hill acted as Robert's primary studio partner on *Fun Trick Noisemaker*, Bill played that role for *New Magnetic Wonder*.

Bill also cowrote the album's opening cut "Can You Feel It?" with Robert, and he would later officially become a band member for *Travellers in Space and Time*. His tragic passing only two years later would prompt Robert to end the Apples in Stereo and change careers.

Looking back now, Robert says, "Those experiences were finite even though they felt infinite at the time." At that moment, Robert felt like he was creating the best work of his life.

"*New Magnetic Wonder* is bursting with experimentalism, sound collages, mathematical musical scales, high-fidelity pop songs, and low-fidelity jams," he enthuses. "It is jangly. It is heavy. It is catchy, and the songs are among my most sensitive. It is our best album."

I have to give Robert points for saying the album *before* his last album is his best album instead of devolving into cliché by saying he "went out on top." It is a considered opinion, even if it isn't an objective one.

Which dots came first? The shirt, the background, or the tie? Actually, the song: "Dots 1-2-3" appears on the debut Apples album Fun Trick Noisemaker. *Following Hilarie's departure, John Dufilho stepped in on drums and Bill Doss of the Olivia Tremor Control joined the band. (L–R): Eric Allen, John Dufilho, Robert Schneider, John Hill, Bill Doss. Photo by Joshua Kessler.*

Robert adds, "*New Magnetic Wonder* also revived the Elephant 6, for better or worse."

That last bit *is* an objective opinion. In addition to Bill, Jeff, and Will Hart all making appearances on the record, and *New Magnetic Wonder* being the first Elephant 6–related release to bear the Elephant 6 logo in years, the album's "Energy" single gave the Apples in Stereo their most consistent run of exposure since the band's alliance with *The Powerpuff Girls* program seven years earlier in 2000.

Along with helping to revive Elephant 6, *New Magnetic Wonder* revived the possibility of the Apples breaking into bigger mainstream success, an idea that leads me back to listening to *New Magnetic Wonder* and *Travellers in Space and Time* in the context presented at the beginning of this book:

If the Apples in Stereo had formed autonomously as bands typically do, would they have found mainstream success in their third decade, independent of their career-long association with the Elephant 6 Recording Co.?

"I am defending *New Magnetic Wonder* because you asked me to."

Even though Robert says that *New Magnetic Wonder* is the band's best album, I can't help but feel, based on the personal nature of our conversations about his life during this period, that he may be overcompensating with optimism in hindsight for the hurt feelings that had to have shadowed the production.

I already knew I would be giving *New Magnetic Wonder* a new listen, but to lighten the mood, I began a fun back-and-forth with Robert in which I asked him to sell me on the album anyway. Not surprisingly, he took the challenge on with vigor.

I joked that I would be calling this chapter "What's It Gonna Take to Get You into *New Magnetic Wonder* Today?" as if he is a sitcom approximation of a used car salesman, but Robert is not that cheesy character. He is an honest dealer who clearly loves his product.

"This album is so epic!" he begins. "It has rabbit holes, and don't forget that I invented a new musical scale that nobody has ever heard before." I suggest that the new musical scale is "nerd bait," and Robert agrees, though, to be fair, this is a conversation between two baited nerds.

"It *is* nerd bait," he says, "but I created a new form of music, and I believe that it will not be lost on the future."

Robert is earnest, and in hindsight I feel a little bad for making him defend his work, but I know he is doing it because he wholeheartedly believes in it. I encourage him to continue his passionate pitch, which is working on me, even though I also continue to push back with my preconceived bias.

Like, why would Robert, whose reputation as a sound-defining producer sits at the top of my "Robert Schneider Ten-Second Elevator Pitch," seek out another producer, Bryce Goggin, who mixed the band's previous album *Velocity of Sound*, and went on to coproduce, engineer, and mix *New Magnetic Wonder*, to achieve his artistic vision?

"I am not capable of a high-fidelity production," Robert admits, and while I would not boast about this on my résumé if I were him, I appreciate the honesty. "It is not in my skills. My vision is not limited, but my skills . . . after I heard [Brian Wilson's] *Smile*, I realized how good a big production could still be, and I wanted to go further. I needed to do hi-fi."

Robert continues to go in on closing the sale by personalizing his tactic with "I know you can appreciate that. I wanted to reach the high-fidelity of something like the late seventies and early eighties as a producer and engineer. I could not do that myself, and I know that you can understand that I wanted that!

"I wanted to reach the level of something like Billy Joel or Queen or Fleetwood Mac, in terms of engineering. I think you can also understand that my bandmates might *not* have wanted that, and that the collective might *not* have appreciated that."

Oh, yes. I do not think that most of the Elephant 6 collective is aspiring to appreciate Billy Joel. No argument there.

"We trusted Bryce," Robert continues. "He recorded Pavement! We couldn't have trusted another engineer. His studio is all in one big room. He doesn't even have a separate control room," Robert explains as part of a respectable effort to illustrate to a skeptical, sometimes cynical, eyebrow-raising dude like me how authentic the recording environment was.

For those unfamiliar with how records are made, sometimes a band will play live in the room together—similar to how they would perform onstage—in order to capture their live intensity. Then they add and record additional parts on top from there.

Despite John Hill being absent from recording basic tracks for *New Magnetic Wonder* because of a Dressy Bessy tour ("I did all of those tracks later in Denver," he explains), Robert says that, typically, "on all of our albums, we always recorded basic tracks live as a band.

"I wanted to get sick live band tracks, recorded through vintage equipment, but in a punk rock room—on Paul McCartney's tape machine!"

In addition to Jeff Mangum's appearance on the album, this factoid seems to have also been overlooked in the marketing of *New Magnetic Wonder*, although Robert justifies it again as something not worth making a big deal about.

"We recorded onto the same tape machine that Paul McCartney once owned. It can be seen on the inner sleeve of *McCartney II*," Robert reveals.

Robert reminds me about his Ampex MM-1200 machine that Bryce picked up in Kentucky and drove back to Brooklyn. Now it sits right next to the McCartney machine in Bryce's studio.

Robert closes his quite convincing explanation for his hi-fi approach to *New Magnetic Wonder* by reminding me that he also "wanted to reach back and make low-fidelity too. The album also contains recordings made on handheld cassette and four-track."

I am still not shaken from the notion that Hilarie's playing, songwriting, and vocals are integral to what THE version of the Apples in Stereo sounds like. My thoughts are stuck in how Hilarie was already thinking about leaving the band at this time.

Then, somehow psychically, Robert brings up "Beautiful Machine," the *New Magnetic Wonder* high point that Hilarie didn't quite remember the name of. When I saw that "Beautiful Machine" is actually a suite titled "Beautiful Machine Parts 1–2" and "Beautiful Machine Parts 3–4," I couldn't wait to listen.

"I hope I will show you why *New Magnetic Wonder* is epic, why it is our most important album, and why it is just as important to Elephant 6 history on the closing side as *Fun Trick Noisemaker* was on the opening side," Robert concludes.

"I make a sales pitch until I close the sale!"

New Magnetic Wonder
New Magnetic Wonder opens with the song Robert and Bill wrote together, "Can You Feel It?"

Bill is quoted in author Kim Cooper's book about *In the Aeroplane Over the Sea* as saying, "I have always been in friendly competition with Robert. He'll send me a batch of songs that'll be so catchy and innovative that I'll have to sit down straightaway and try to show him up by writing something better. Of course, I never have been able to best him, but it has spawned many of what I consider my best songs."

It is wonderful listening to "Can You Feel It?" with this knowledge.

"Drown out the bullshit on the FM radio!" Robert sings, sounding like he is inhaling the mic and breathing out the fire he is filled with. Suddenly, the music drops out save for an insistent pulse, and in its place we are consumed by a cacophony of voices, before we return to the song and are driven to its conclusion with a repetition of "Turn up the stereo!"

It is a literal command and a metaphorical one.

The song concludes with what initially sounds like location audio of a club concert audience cheering, but then one of the audience members angrily shouts, "Turn it down! Turn it down! Everything's feedbacking! Can't you hear it?!"

"We had played in Manchester the night before and because of traffic it took us eight hours to get to the venue," John Hill explains of the field recording, which was made on November 6, 2002, at 93 Feet East in London.

"We barely had time to set up and only sound-checked for one song. Robert and I both had Vox AC30 amps that we weren't used to using because it was only the second show of the tour. It was the only time I can remember that I was ready to fight someone in the crowd!"

"Can You Feel It?" also showcases the nimble muscularity

of Eric's bass playing and is once again an immediate reminder that Hilarie's background vocals can never be replaced.

I realize now that I have been writing for months leading up to this listening and less than two minutes in, it feels cathartic. The moment is like finally meeting someone that I have been enthusiastically told about for so long. I am on my first date with *New Magnetic Wonder* and this record better pick up the check!

Apple Picking, Pt. Fourteen
"Skyway" from *New Magnetic Wonder*

"'Skyway' sounds different from other Apples songs," Eric says. This *New Magnetic Wonder* track is another one from the band's catalog that immediately came to Eric's mind. "It has this consistent drive that seems different, and the single-note piano part is very Stooges."

"Elijah didn't like the piano on 'Skyway,'" Robert says. I include this quote to once again remind that despite the kind of evidence that may indicate a sellout—a "grab at the ring"—Robert did not capitulate to the will of billion-dollar corporations or the stars of billion-dollar-grossing movie franchises.

If there were artistic compromises happening, they were due to Robert's life experiences, not existential ones. It is supremely difficult for any record by any band to encapsulate the passion, hunger, and desperation that comes with early recordings when you just want someone—anyone—to hear and to care.

I don't envy any artist that seeks to summon and suffer the life challenges required to make substantial work post-success.

"Skyway" is the sound of a seasoned live band playing in that career period between mastery and starting to just go through the motions. In only two minutes and forty seconds, the Apples get as close to a perfect Pavement song as Pavement ever got.

"Maybe you should do the whole book on 'Skyway!'" Eric suggests. "I've heard Robert work on many songs over the years. Sometimes I've heard them evolve as he thinks and strums until he lands on the right melody or the right lyrics. Or he might present something at practice or sound check or in the van or in the hotel room that would pretty much be a finished song. 'Skyway' is unique."

"I think that all of my favorite songs come from dreams," Robert says. "I wrote 'Skyway' in a dream, and I woke up right afterwards and put it down."

Eric continues, "Robert played me the fully realized song with these lyrics that are direct, yet have a mysterious, accusatory vagueness. The lyrics still puzzle me. I love every line in this song, and as someone who loves a futile pursuit, trying to crack the hidden meaning of 'Skyway' is an enduring favorite."

> *Forty lessons you may hear from the sun, now*
> *You never listened to a single one*
> *Falling leaves whisper like thieves*
> *Not that you mind you live on stolen time*
> —"Skyway"

"Robert told me he had a dream where he was arrested and was sitting in the police station with an officer. There was a radio on, it was playing the Velvet Underground, and

Robert told the officer to turn it up," Eric remembers.

"Eric's account of 'Skyway' is uncannily accurate," Robert says. "There was this magical nostalgic house party with everyone I have ever known.

"The party spilled out into the street and the police came. I ended up facing a police officer who enthused to me about a song by the Velvet Underground that I hadn't heard. It was playing on a single monophonic speaker at the end of the table."

Eric adds, "The radio was small with a silver face, a tiny speaker, and a chrome antenna. I pictured an *Andy Griffith Show* sort of small-town police station. Robert isn't handcuffed, and there is an open case full of shotguns in the background, but everyone including the criminals are honorable, so there is no cause for concern.

"Nothing changed from what Robert played for me that day to the completed recorded version on *New Magnetic Wonder*," Eric says. "We learned it and started playing it live for a while before we recorded it. I just love the song."

"It was a very beautiful dream," Robert concludes.

The short interstitial musical segments spread throughout *New Magnetic Wonder* call back to the 1999 release *Her Wallpaper Reverie*, although their use on that record was often criticized as a shortcoming at the time.

As it was then, these pieces represent the "art" aspect of the "all three" Apples, but they contribute to a disconnectedness that I feel like I am forced to narratively attribute to the band actually unraveling at the time.

As a lead-in to "Energy," however, the thirty-four second "Mellotron 1" works like a decent bait and switch, as in,

"Let's give 'em some 'art,' and then wallop 'em with some 'as pop as we get.'"

Apple Picking, Pt. Fifteen
"Energy" from *New Magnetic Wonder*

"I wrote 'Energy' for Max as he was drifting off to sleep when he was five or six," Robert recalls. "I put him to bed, and the sun was setting, and I went out on our porch, which was just outside his bedroom window, in our backyard.

"I was playing guitar, and I was aware of the fact that he might hear it. I decided to write a song that would mean something to him, and express what I believe to him. So I started to sing about energy.

"I wrote it for Max, so I am very happy and proud that it is my most popular song, because it is his song."

Does Max know "Energy" was written for him?

"Yes, he does!" Robert answers. "He used to play it with me live sometimes when he was younger."

"Ever since I started teaching, back in 2013, on my last day of math class, I have had a party with snacks and a surprise musical guest," Robert describes. "Of course, the guest is me, and I play 'Energy' for my students. It's basically the only time I regularly play guitar now that I'm a mathematician. I tell my students how I wrote the song for Max, who is now their age, and for their generation."

Robert believes that "Energy" became the most popular song by the Apples in Stereo because it was written with so much love, and that the love must be encoded in the recording somehow. He might be right. Like good cooking made with love, "Energy" was not only written with love but recorded with love too.

"Bill and I sang the backing vocals for 'Energy' with our arms around each other in his attic studio," Robert recalls. "Bill and I usually recorded harmonies that way. I miss that."

Romantic love plays a role in the story of how "Energy" became ubiquitous too.

Remember: "Pepsi was our choice, photos were not!"

"Marci said 'Energy' reminded her of the Coca-Cola anthem, 'I'd Like to Teach the World to Sing (In Perfect Harmony),'" Robert says. "In our generation, that Coca-Cola song was like heaven. It presented a very seventies view of humanity holding hands all together. That still speaks to me. When I wrote 'Energy,' my friends thought everybody would sing it, so I had that sort of ambition. Pepsi got their own nice song."

As for the previously mentioned music video for "Energy," Robert says, "Elijah wanted to direct something, and his friends had these Super 8 cameras. It was basically made for free. We set up in his friend's loft. It was kind of a warehouse in the Dumbo area of Brooklyn."

Nothing speaks louder than a comments section. The marketing muscle behind "Energy" is summed up this way: "They play this damn song all the time at the mall where I live!" reads one comment on YouTube.

I don't disagree with "damn song."

"Energy" could easily become annoying, and ironically, it is actual energy that I miss. The song isn't without it, but the hunger of 1995 is missing.

The effects of success on art are inescapable, but an artist can only create as the person they are now. Experiences cannot be undone, and so when I allow myself to go where the production takes me, I get it. It is easy to forget that so much of what Robert does is about creating a sonic world, as Eric said earlier.

Robert is not typically thought of as a singer-songwriter, at least not in the same sense as Jeff Mangum, for example, a "proper" singer-songwriter whom Robert will forever be associated with. "Energy" being the biggest song that Robert has ever written contributes to this narrative because of the tune's production-based nature and success as a sales tool for a soft drink.

It is a bizarre contrast when considered against the rest of Robert's career, where he has found the majority of his success serving the most vulnerable, unhinged, and chance-taking work of others, mainly through his groundbreaking production for Neutral Milk Hotel and the Olivia Tremor Control.

Bizarre as the suggestion of that contrast may be, the success of "Energy" is reality.

"It is our flagship song, and I think it will likely represent our band in the future," Robert concludes.

"Same Old Drag" feels like the intersection of the innocence of Charles Schulz's *Peanuts* and the abandon of Dizzy Gillespie's "Salt Peanuts."

The production on *New Magnetic Wonder* is absolutely alluring. Robert's little sonic trick-or-treats appear throughout and are his trademark at this point. I wouldn't mind at all if a vocoder was not one of them.

You are better than this much vocoder, Robert!

I am reminded of the swirling production touches noted earlier on "Benefits of Lying (With Your Friend)" from *Her Wallpaper Reverie* that the performance by the kid on TikTok revealed as unnecessary.

I want to hear more of Robert's sensitive songwriting, but when the overt production is working, it works overtime. If there is a pathway to proclaiming *New Magnetic Wonder* a masterpiece, it is in Robert's arrival as a singular visionary as far as manifesting what he imagines emerging from the studio monitors. These sounds are sumptuous.

Moving on amid Jeff's sloppy drum fills—maybe this is why Robert chose not to draw attention to him—Hilarie intones with her unmistakable vocals, pulling off the rare, almost impossible feat of having defined a unique voice on the indie pop underground. Christian Hoard, writing for NPR, said about Hilarie's "Sunndal Song": "Rarely is guitar pop done this well."

Hilarie's songwriting in the High Water Marks shows she has only improved since *New Magnetic Wonder*, which is saying a lot since she has been showing off her skills all along, albeit without enough space to display them. Refer back to chapter 7 for just a few highlights.

I desperately want to forget that Hilarie is about to leave the band when I hear "Sunndal Song." The behind-the-scenes reality hangs over the entire record. Robert tries to muzzle the vocoder until the end of the track, but he eventually gives in.

"Deep" Robert arrives just in time on "Play Tough." It is one of the tracks that Hilarie mentioned as a highlight of *New Magnetic Wonder*.

> *Saturday you woke me up into a drag*
> *Peaches in the creases of a plastic bag*
> *Saturday is not the ideal day to break up*
> *Don't you know it takes a little time to wake up*
> —"Play Tough"

Robert's enunciation of "my love" throughout the song intentionally adds cinematic-style drama each time he sings it. "Play Tough" is where I want the Apples in Stereo to lean when they make their comeback record. I will continue this wishful thinking in chapter 10.

Robert is smart to sequence "Sun Is Out" next. The song starts in intimate lo-fi mode before growing into a campfire atmosphere accompanied by a punctuated McCartney-style bass line. In fact, the entire production of the track is not unlike an ode out of respect to the *McCartney II* tape machine in the room.

We already talked about the non-Pythagorean scale nerd bait. In my ears, it sounds as if I am being given a hearing test. I pass it but almost pass out.

If "Skyway" is the Apples in Stereo as Pavement, "7 Stars" is the Apples in Stereo as Sonic Youth gone psych. The song is another that Hilarie mentioned as a *New Magnetic Wonder* favorite.

Robert also cited "7 Stars" as one of his proud moments as a rock guitarist. While I want to slap the vocoder out of Robert's hands at this point, I don't want to inflict any more pain.

> *Simple lives we once left behind*
> *We're so distracted now*
> *Secret lives we have lived inside*
> *We're going backwards now*
> —"7 Stars"

The version of "Radiation" on *New Magnetic Wonder,* recorded in Bill Doss's attic studio, is already *so* sad. A decade and change after Bill's passing, it is gut-wrenching watching

Robert perform "Radiation" solo on acoustic guitar in 2023 during the Q&A session mentioned earlier following the premiere of the Elephant 6 documentary in New York City.

Rolling Stone correctly called the song "gorgeous" in its review of *New Magnetic Wonder*.

At the outset of his acoustic performance in New York, Robert says it is the first time he has performed in a year. His mournful voice comes to life, paying tribute to his best friend who can be seen on-screen just over Robert's shoulder as he sings.

> *You gotta get back to the place that you know you're gonna see your friends again*
> —"Radiation"

I am breathing a deep sigh for "deep" Robert.

"It's the greatest moment of the Apples jamming loudly!"

Robert is referring to the four-part suite "Beautiful Machine Parts 1–2" and "Beautiful Machine Parts 3–4" that essentially end *New Magnetic Wonder*.

"'Beautiful Machine' was recorded as one long live piece," Robert explains. "We recorded all four parts back-to-back live in one take! Instead of playing in the drum booth, Hilarie played in the room with us, so it has a room sound."

It is good to know Robert was aware Hilarie was in the room and that she didn't just set up her drums behind his back.

But seriously.

I am a sucker for song-naming conceits like this, and in both its construction, and later in its sound, I was reminded of Neutral Milk Hotel's "King of Carrot Flowers" suite.

Robert explains, "Originally, 'King of Carrot Flowers Pt. 1' and 'King of Carrot Flowers Pts. 2 & 3' were separate songs that Jeff tied together conceptually when he was making the storyline of the album. I think it's a natural device to use, from classical music and such, and also a natural psychedelic, prog, and pretentious thing to do."

I immediately knew why this four-part piece was on Hilarie's mind, and I was immediately impressed when I listened to all seven minutes and thirty-six seconds of it.

"Listen to the end of it as it builds, and the Mellotron comes in," Robert instructs. "The live band is really heavy! We are together and getting that heavy sludgy feel, just like at band practice."

> *Oh, don't you know it's right*
> *We will live together for a long time*
> *Oh, don't you know it's wrong*
> *We will be forgotten when we're gone*
> —"Beautiful Machine Parts 3–4"

"I hope I will show you why *New Magnetic Wonder* is epic, and why it is our most important album," Robert said earlier.

Hilarie in the room makes all the difference. The intensity of this nearly eight-minute section of *New Magnetic Wonder* pushes it to "epic" proportions. There is no other word, really.

Then, I remember what else Robert said earlier: "She was like thunder onstage. Epic."

The surprising, insistent, and intense spark that Hilarie brought to this band plays in past tense as "Beautiful

Machine Parts 3–4" crescendos. Strings are introduced in the final minutes. Minutes that feel like they could repeat on a loop infinitely as *New Magnetic Wonder* comes to a close, along with Hilarie's tenure in the Apples in Stereo.

Actually, the word "tenure" makes it sound as if Hilarie served time, like serving a prison sentence. No way. Hilarie serves time like a drummer serves time, and she goes out serving it like a motherfucker on "Beautiful Machine Parts 3–4."

Now I long to hear this song live!

When idealistic young people come together to do something extraordinary, that extraordinary experience often turns idealistic young people into people they weren't before.

When that phase of the journey is complete, and a new journey begins, some people choose to go on the new journey together, and some are satisfied with the way it used to be and decline to embrace the way it no longer is.

The divide between Hilarie's perception of her role on *New Magnetic Wonder* and Robert's remembrance of it is not unlike the "She's Just Like Me" cymbal controversy from earlier. Robert offers his perspective with grace, even amid what feels like a tense exchange on the topic.

"Hilarie is a hero of our band and also a hero of indie rock. We made *New Magnetic Wonder* together," Robert says of the time leading up to Hilarie leaving. "Recording sessions, band practices, and tours . . . all together.

"Hilarie quitting the band was not desired."

Regardless of my characterization of a band mired in turmoil, which is based on basic ideas about human nature and my specific conversations with the band members, Robert says, "I had all of my friends on *New Magnetic*

Wonder. It is like looking at a photo album of happy memories and happy places when I listen to it."

I believe him.

Jann Wenner's unfortunate Joni Mitchell slight from earlier notwithstanding, it is worth noting that *Rolling Stone* placed *New Magnetic Wonder* at no. 28 on the magazine's "Top 50 Albums of 2007" list.

Robert may be such an intense mathematical intellect that he has performed the calculations required to successfully plug my preconceived bias about *New Magnetic Wonder* and *Travellers in Space and Time* into an evolutionary equation that resolves my resistance to the albums in question.

Clearly, it worked so far on how I am now hearing *New Magnetic Wonder.*

Travellers in Space and Time would arrive in 2010 with some exceedingly professional photo shoots preceding it. These approved (not tossed in the bin!) images featuring the latest lineup of the Apples (Robert, Eric, Bill, John, John, and John) prompt the question—is the Apples in Stereo the only band ever to contain three members named John?

Some of the photos of the era depict the band in a "costumed" look, donning smart, matching futuristic outfits. Others have Robert wearing a robe, his eyes behind wraparound shades that he would also be seen wearing onstage.

Visuals, including the music video we will discuss shortly, can look dated as time passes, and then more time passes, and they look fashionable again. Only later did it occur to me that Robert's late 2000s "robe" look seemed somehow inspired by Brian Wilson's physical appearance during his darkest days of living in seclusion with his doctor.

The new images accompanied the slickest sound the Apples had ever offered. I appreciate that Robert reinvented the band on *Travellers in Space and Time*. He had to, and it is his inclination and right as an artist anyway. Does the post-Hilarie version of the Apples in Stereo make me dismissively say, "No way!?" As always, the music, fixed in perpetuity, is all that matters. Let's listen.

Travellers in Space and Time

"Max and I were mutually obsessed over the album *Time* by Electric Light Orchestra back then," Robert explains.

It comes as no surprise that the vocals on opener "Dream About the Future" immediately remind me of Jeff Lynne of Electric Light Orchestra. In addition to Jeff Lynne, thoughts of Wayne Coyne of the Flaming Lips (an early tour mate of the Apples) and Andy Partridge of XTC (whom Robert worked with on an aborted collaboration) linger.

Even so, those latter singers don't serve as indicators of just how production-focused *Travellers in Space and Time* is.

The "more cowbell" of "Hey Elevator" firmly announces, "*Travellers in Space and Time* is a dance record!" The influence of Kool & the Gang is in the house and serving grooves so smooth that I can almost give Robert a pass on the ever-present vocoder that has carried itself over from *New Magnetic Wonder*.

Almost.

"R&B is my favorite form," Robert says. "It was never understood by my Elephant 6 friends."

The aesthetic of *Travellers* is very specific, and potentially polarizing, but it gives an impression of Robert as a songwriting shape-shifter who could have pulled off a Barry Gibb during this era by writing hits for other artists, like what the eldest Gibb did for Barbra Streisand, Dionne Warwick, and Kenny Rogers & Dolly Parton, except Robert would offer up his novel hyperkinetic R&B style.

I have a feeling that a development like this would be about as appreciated by the collective as Robert aspiring to Billy Joel–level production, but apparently some of the cool kids could handle it!

Surprisingly, *Pitchfork* finally came around, giving a generally positive review to *Travellers in Space and Time*. The piece by writer Paul Thompson rightfully points out the album's focus on production, and while characterizing the disco leanings of the record as "more Leo Sayer than Donna Summer" is an over-the-top white-boy slight, Paul seems to get what Robert is going for.

Thompson later comments, "As ever, these songs aren't the deepest lyrically: Schneider's more concerned with achieving a classic sound, which results in a lot of universal sentiment that can at times border on the trite."

If you have learned anything so far, it is that this perception of Robert's songwriting has a basis in fact, but is mainly perception. Perception is reality, however, and so let's continue to change the perception!

Much of Robert's songwriting is overlooked because of his complex productions. When critics talk about songs being "buried in production," they are typically saying a record is overproduced. In the case of *Travellers*, instead of being buried in production, the record is buried in producer!

The fair and fairly candid review of *Travellers in Space and Time* from *Pitchfork* leans positive *because* of its focus on the production of the album, which presents Robert at the height of his powers. It has been quite a journey from nowhere to here!

Despite the popularity of "Energy" as the band's most successful song, John Hill says that another track from the era most represents the Apples in Stereo at this time.

"[The years] 2007 through 2010 seem to be defined by 'Dance Floor,'" he says. "*New Magnetic Wonder* was actually the bridge between the old and the new. You could hear the new coming, but it wasn't fully realized until *Travellers in Space and Time*."

Apple Picking, Pt. Sixteen
"Dance Floor" from *Travellers in Space and Time*

"Did I tell you about Dan's response to "Dance Floor"?

Ironically, the "trite" perception that *Pitchfork* notes regarding Robert's lyrics on *Travellers in Space and Time* is probably what excited the band's manager Daniel Efram into thinking about "Dance Floor" as potentially the band's biggest hit.

On the surface, the song sounds made for the dance floor, and if you're actually on the dance floor, you're not looking for more than that.

"He was blown away," Robert remembers. "He was grooving so hard on it. He loved it so much! I've never seen him so happy and excited. I could practically see him imagining us in the Top 40. He hugged me, and said, 'I'm so proud of you, Robert!' And then I got to the chorus."

Suddenly, "deep" Robert, the one who is so often overlooked, dropped the lyric and let Dan down.

The dance floor isn't there no more

But my body's still moving
—"Dance Floor"

"Dan stopped cold. He shook his head a little bit. His face turned from happy to angry. He looked at me and barked, "The dance floor isn't there no more!? I can't dance to that!"

Robert's description of Dan's reaction reminds me of Robert's glee regarding Jeff Price's panicked phone call about how *Velocity of Sound* made him think his car speakers were blown out.

Dan comments, "It was a ribbing only. Robert had produced such a catchy song, but it had a sad side as well. I'm certain we hugged afterwards!"

Robert agrees, "We did hug! Dan was poking fun, it's true, but he was also irritated."

In Dan's defense, a music industry executive I trust once summed up the plight of band managers to me this way: "None of the glory, all of the blame."

I can imagine, as Robert did, that Dan saw a glimpse of the Apples in Stereo playing every card they had ever accumulated, surpassing the accomplishments of "Energy," and securing the biggest hit of their career.

In an instant, Dan's glimpse was dashed.

"The dance floor isn't there no more" seemed to undermine what the song purported to be—a dance floor anthem—but the very next line arrives with a save.

I point out that the lyric that follows, "But my body's still moving," provides plenty of what is needed to keep the room jumping, but apparently it is one line too late.

"Yes, exactly!" Robert agrees. "Things changed, but I didn't."

Robert's confirmation helps anchor "Dance Floor" in a more emotionally resonant place than it existed moments before, and as if to drive the point home, Robert adds, "When I play it live, I play it acoustically, very slow, very sad, and solemn."

Indeed, the acoustic version of the song, which Robert performed at the same IFC Center screening of *The Elephant 6 Recording Co.* documentary discussed earlier, sheds light on the "art" of the songwriting by offering a less shrouded presentation of the essential idea of personal resilience in the face of unending life changes and challenges contained in those two lines.

The fully produced version of "Dance Floor" as it appears on *Travellers in Space and Time* makes Dan's initial reaction to it no mystery. It is pretty impossible not to "groove so hard on it," "love it so much," and say, "I'm so proud of you, Robert!"

Of course, it would be odd for the average fan to say out loud, "I'm so proud of you, Robert!" while listening, but in its own way, dancing to a song you are motivated to move to is actually an expression of pride.

If "Dance Floor" does not define this era of the Apples in Stereo, as John Hill previously stated, it is at least the conceptual centerpiece of *Travellers*, as further evidenced by the promotional efforts surrounding the song.

As with the still images of the band at this time, the music and promo videos accompanying "Dance Floor" offer a definitive point of view, for better or worse.

The concept music video for "Dance Floor" stars Elijah Wood, whose Simian Records label released *Travellers in Space and Time* as it had done with *New Magnetic Wonder*. Elijah appears in the video as the host of the fictional "Exploring the Universe with Elijah Wood" science education program, watching himself interviewing Robert in full character as "Dr. Robert Schneider," years before Robert actually earned his PhD in mathematics.

The "interview" that Elijah is watching was culled from an actual five-minute "episode" of the *Exploring the Universe with Elijah Wood* show, produced for this purpose. It is full of somewhat forced-feeling puns and references to previous records by the Apples. The device that "Dr. Schneider" introduces that "enables us to travel through space and time" is named "E.L.F.N.T. - 6," for example, which a skeptical, sometimes cynical, eyebrow-raising dude like me rolls his eyes at, but seems to please people in the comments section, which is where it counts.

I have a hard time imagining Hilarie participating in a video with such a self-referential shift in tone, but not imagining it may be the point. To understand the Apples in Stereo at this stage of the band's existence, it means applying the bigger lesson learned above: An artist can only create as the person they are now. Hilarie took a vibe with her when she left, to be sure, but a new vibe proposes when another vibe closes.

Robert in this era is fascinated with production, and he is becoming fascinated with the math of production. He became fascinated with math *because* of production when he found himself forced to regularly fix his tape machine. So it is not surprising he is portrayed as a "mad scientist" in the "Dance Floor" music video. He fits the bill, and in all our perceptions of the world around us we look for what fits the bill.

Beneath the bill, it is sort of jarring that even at the end of fifteen-plus years of making Apples in Stereo music, a song that would seem like a purely fun throwaway dance-party jam, which is literally titled "Dance Floor," is actually very sad, to the point where the band's manager, when asked for a comment about having his dreams of a hit song dashed by the lyrics, mentions that specific detail.

Again, "Robert had produced such a catchy song, but it had a sad side as well."

I completely agree with all the assessments that everyone always makes about Robert, in that he is an incredibly effusive, encouraging, and enigmatic character, but I also know that a lot of that, while being absolutely genuine and authentic, is also a genuine and authentic development of a part of his personality built to counter the sadness that is ultimately heard in his songs.

The fact that the band's final big single is *not* a purely fun throwaway dance-party jam is a big reason to revisit and reevaluate the band's catalog, or to dig deep into it for the first time. You will see that the Apples in Stereo are "all three."

Apple Picking, Pt. Seventeen
"No One in the World" from *Travellers in Space and Time*
"No One in the World" is a brilliant Brill-Building-by-way-of-Broadway-style special with an addictive bouncy piano figure that is unfortunately interrupted by. . .vocoder. I am actually angry at the overuse of vocoder now.

Was Robert being threatened with bodily harm by the vocoder mafia?

"It was conceptual," Robert explains after receiving an irate text from me about it. "No one used it then, except Daft Punk. Now, it's everywhere."

John Dufilho's drumming here is the first time it is clear that I hear an Apples song where Hilarie would not be the most appropriate player. "No One in the World" calls for straightforward crispy time without an overemphasis on style (no shade!), and that is what Dufilho delivers, locked in the pocket with PRE.

Robert sings like he's in love, backed by a soulful, stabbing horn section laying down some nasty business as they appropriately perform a perfectly synchronized dance break in my imagination. "No One in the World" is the most legit groove Robert has ever walked out of a studio with.

While listening, I said out loud without thinking, "Robert would have never written a song like this for the Apples in Stereo," and if that unfiltered thought isn't testament to the difference embedded in my mind between THE version and this version of the band, I don't know what is.

As it turns out, my impulsive thought about Robert not writing this song has a basis in reality.

"Van Dyke Parks almost wrote the lyrics for 'No One in the World,'" Robert tells me of the legendary songwriter best known for his collaborations with the Beach Boys, Lowell George of Little Feat, Harry Nilsson, and many more. "I met him at the BIGSOUND Festival in Australia, and we hung out a lot!

"When we discussed the collaboration, the only lyric I had was for the chorus—*There's no one in the world like my little girl*—but Van told me he needs to ride with no lyrics at all or else it interferes with his spontaneity and creativity, which I totally understand."

"No One in the World" is not "Dance Floor" hot, it is stone-cold. This is what the Elephant *Sex* Collective would sound like to the friends who "never understood" that R&B is Robert's "favorite form."

The self-referential moments described earlier continue as we see the Elephant 6 logo featured on the neck of Robert's guitar in the music video for the song "Told You Once." Skeptical, sometimes cynical, eyebrow-raising dudes like me are, once again, confronted by the comments section telling us what's happening on the streets.

"Told You Once" has also made the mall scene, like "Energy" did previously. "They play this song in Forever 21 all the time!" reads one comment. The commenter doesn't seem to mind one bit.

In fact, the internet comment community is generally positive about both *New Magnetic Wonder* and *Travellers in Space and Time*. It is as if the higher visibility for both records has served to cultivate a contingent of new fans of the Apples in Stereo that take these songs at face value without knowing, or ever caring about, the history of the band or the music that came before.

Please refer back to chapter 6 for an in-depth discussion of Eric's standout *Travellers* tune "Next Year at About the Same Time." Sung by Bill Doss, it is the album's most legitimately reverential and welcomed nod to the Elephant 6 sound.

I asked myself previously if my preconceived bias against *New Magnetic Wonder* and *Travellers in Space and Time* was reasonable. The answer is irrelevant now because I have formed a post-conceived bias and have come to the conclusion that both states of mind can exist.

My skepticism about *New Magnetic Wonder* and

Travellers, based on what looked like Robert's blatant careerism amid Hilarie leaving the band, is valid.

My experience savoring both these records is also valid. We can form a preconceived bias based on a certain set of parameters and form a post-conceived bias based on a new set of parameters. It's only art, after all!

When Hilarie left the Apples in Stereo, I thought I saw Robert's previously held "I gave up nothing" posture start to give way to a focus on attempting to make the band more popular by compromising standards and "grabbing at the ring" of success. I completely understood that impulse, but my heart would not allow me to understand the resulting art.

Not one person listens to a record and says to themselves, "I would have liked this song more if it were marketed differently." But when artists are in the process of creating work, professional and personal life circumstances are embedded into whatever ends up pressed on vinyl. No matter what we think we see, what we hear is evidence of the truth of the time.

The same goes for listeners. I will never get to find out what my actual impression was of *New Magnetic Wonder* and *Travellers in Space and Time* in 2007 and 2010 when these records were released. Today, I hear those truths of the time, as pressed into the platters. They are moving, and they make me move.

With this in mind, maybe my kvetching about vocoders will lessen in time.

I said that I snap-judge art without thinking. In this chapter, I learned to slow-judge. There is great value in taking time to consider the work in the context of the life that the artist was living at the moment of creation, instead of the life they were living before or after.

What does John Lennon's *Plastic Ono Band* sound like separated from the Beatle history that has always colored my immediate perception? I look forward to finding out!

When heroes who are legends (like Lennon) or friends who are heroes (like Bill Doss and Will Hart) pass away, their work is fixed in time, and now so are their lives. The artist cannot speak to the listener's ever-evolving perceptions of the work that speaks for itself.

The lived experiences of the members of the Apples in Stereo continue to accumulate. The work is fixed and done, but perhaps the perception has just begun?

Robert said, "It is like looking at a photo album of happy memories and happy places . . . I miss that."

Perhaps the Apples in Stereo ended prematurely.

10. POST-CONCEIVED BIAS: "LET ME TELL YOU 'BOUT THE END OF THE BEGINNING"

Text from Robert Schneider, March 18, 2025, at 9:31 a.m.: "Very private, but I'm sending this to you as I send it to Max. Demo of a new song I wrote that he is going to play with me at Will Hart's memorial in two weeks. Recorded last night on my Voice Memo app."

Robert's best friend and Elephant 6 Recording Co. cofounder Will Hart of the Olivia Tremor Control died on November 29, 2024, at the age of fifty-three.

At a celebration of Will's life that took place on March 29, 2025, in Athens, Georgia, at the famed 40 Watt Club, Robert performed the new song that he shared with me over text on March 18.

I was emotionally struck by "Night Train" even before pressing play, and overwhelmingly so as I heard Robert's acoustic guitar and then his singing voice, which I realized I had not heard on a new song in so long. Robert's unique tone rises tenderly as he sings goodbye to his lifelong friend.

I was brought to tears by the subject matter, but more so as I found myself touched by the real voice of the real Robert I know.

Many fans hope for Robert to reconnect with writing

songs and making music in this straightforward way, or at least more straightforward than various appearances on records with friends and associates allow. These days, Robert writes songs when he feels like it, but he doesn't record them anymore.

"I just don't have the emotional energy to engineer since Bill Doss passed away."

As mentioned in chapter 7, Robert's musical output recently has been relegated to his ongoing interest in generative AI. While the loss of Bill turned Robert away from seeking comfort, or at least an outlet, through music-making, the passing of Robert's family cat of seventeen years brought him back.

"When Odd passed away, I used the AI website Suno to generate about a thousand instrumental tracks as therapy," he says.

Unintentionally, Robert's cat named Odd made Robert an odd duck among artist peers when it came to his embrace of generative AI to make music.

Most reject it with a passion and make their voices heard—John Darnielle of the Mountain Goats comes to mind—when Robert lightheartedly defends his work and process. I am not as dismissive of this work as some, but it does motivate me to encourage more work like "Night Train."

There is more for Robert to say the old-fashioned way.

Robert's use of generative AI fulfills him on some level artistically, so it is purely selfish on my part to wish for him to leverage the tragedies he has endured for entertainment purposes. Perhaps he has been confronted by so much loss that it leads him to use this particular tool because composing songs that mirror this pain back to him is overwhelming.

Leaving the Apples behind after Bill's death is a pretty clear indicator of his mindset.

Robert's harsh realities find their way into his AI work as much as they possibly can considering the limitations of the technology to actually express an artist's feelings. Even though prompts are the output of a biological prompter, and using the word "disappointed" is too damn harsh considering the circumstances, I still want to hear songs that reflect the realities of Robert's latest lived life.

It is astounding from a purely objective standpoint for one person to have experienced so much loss among the group of collaborators who created so much personal gain. The friends Robert grew up with—and tied his artistic legacy and even his persona to before he became a mathematician—died young (Bill Doss and Will Hart) or became estranged (Jeff Mangum) amid feelings of betrayal (my word, not Robert's).

Perhaps there is another chapter in Robert's artistic story that will make sense of this. Perhaps a solo album written and recorded in the legendary singer-songwriter tradition. Perhaps Robert's history of studying Buddhism contributes to the strength and methods by which he manages tragedy, and can therefore influence his work in the future. I am not being overly sympathetic. I already admitted I am selfish!

Hopefully, "Night Train" is the beginning of sharing some sort of catharsis.

Text from Robert Schneider, March 28, 2025, at 11:01 a.m.: "Private recording :) Me and Max practicing in his bedroom for the memorial show."

On March 28, the day before the celebration in Athens,

I heard from Robert about "Night Train" again. This time, a practice session, recorded in twenty-four-year-old Max's bedroom. Max is accompanying his father by lending a delicate lead guitar line that similarly guts me. So thoughtful and representative of the underpinnings of the band that Max's mother and father brought into the world.

The implications of the cyclical familial nature of it all contribute to the emotional power of "Night Train," no doubt, but objectively it's a great composition by Robert that reminds of what he is still capable of artistically when the stakes are high.

> *Let me tell you 'bout the end of the beginning*
> *Or of the end, depends on where you land*
> *You came on the scene just as the plot is thinning*
> *I'll start again, and then you'll understand*
> —"The Bird That You Can't See"

I commented on our text thread that the house would be in tears when they heard "Night Train," and Robert sidestepped my compliment to let me know about a correctly termed "*almost* Apples reunion" that would take place that evening.

"When I realized Fuzz and PRE would be there, I asked them if they would play during my set time that I had allotted for me and Max at the memorial show," Robert says.

Eric adds, "We didn't make a plan to go to Athens and play, but realized that Robert, John, and I were all going to be there. I can't imagine any of us not going to celebrate Will Hart if we have the ways and means to.

"There was obviously sadness about the occasion, and about what this brilliant night of music and performance was for," Eric continues. "It helped me that it was a few months after Will's passing. I was able to deal with the shock and grief and explosive tears at home before needing to be in public and around friends."

Not even the fact that Robert had to perform on a strange guitar could mess with the moment.

Robert at Trout Recording in Brooklyn during the making of New Magnetic Wonder. *Fun fact: The glasses he's wearing were destroyed on the set of the Mike Myers film* The Love Guru, *in which Robert played a cameo role as a banjo player in a bluegrass band. Yes, this actually happened! Photo by Adam Cantor.*

"Robert stressed that he hadn't played guitar in two years, and had to relearn the songs," Eric explains. "I wasn't worried about us playing together after a long hiatus, however. Within minutes on a borrowed Stratocaster—I can't remember seeing Robert ever play a Strat—he sounded like Robert Schneider."

"It was really special to be able to get together and play," John offers. "It had an impromptu feel, but I think all three of us remembered we have a special bond personally and onstage. It's times like these that drive home how special your partners are, whether it's partners in life or partners in song."

Eric agrees, saying, "When we get together, it sounds like the Apples."

Hilarie expressed her grief in a public post on Facebook, saying, "When Will lived in our apartment in Denver I learned to see the world and art in a new way. I'm forever grateful. He is probably the most unique and original person that I've had the pleasure to know. I'm so sad that he's left our realm."

Although Hilarie was also very close with Will, it was highly unlikely that she would fly over from Norway to attend the memorial. If she had, the "*almost* Apples reunion" would most certainly have been actual.

With Max in attendance, how could Robert and Hilarie back away from the opportunity for their son to watch his parents play "Energy," the song his dad wrote for him?

Following Robert and Max's emotional performance of "Night Train," Robert was joined onstage by John Hill, Eric Allen, and others at the 40 Watt Club to perform three Apples songs.

The surprise short set, which included the live staples "Stream Running Over" and "Energy," was especially notable for featuring the first-ever live performance of "The Silvery Light of a Dream" and "The Silvery Light of a Dream Pt. 2" from 1997's *Tone Soul Evolution*, now forever known as the album Seymour Stein signed to Sire Records over spaghetti.

"It was cool to do something 'new' for Will's tribute," Eric says. "It is such a beautiful song that I hadn't thought about because we never played it live."

Robert reveals, "I think my best song is 'The Silvery Light of a Dream.' Both parts."

Robert introduces the song from the stage at Will's memorial by dedicating it to Bill Doss and repeating that he thinks it's his best song.

He later tells me, "It has my best lyrics. They are for my grandmother and express something hard to say out loud."

The importance of this song to Robert—its meaning so powerful that he backs away from discussing it too deeply, and the fact that it was never played live in the nearly thirty years since it was recorded—speaks again to the emotional weight of the catalog of this "pop" band, that is actually "all three."

"When I meet people out in the wild who were too young to have experienced the Apples in Stereo the first time around, but discovered us later," Eric says, "I'm always a little shocked, and always very happy."

Is this chapter meant to suggest a reunion tour by the Apples in Stereo featuring a full album performance of *Fun Trick Noisemaker* along with a supplemental set list of essential Apples songs?

Yes!

I just hope that whoever is hired to handle sound has the crash cymbal miking scenario for "She's Just Like Me" settled and squared away long before it launches.

When enough time has passed to have perspective on wounds that may not have completely healed but no longer hurt, then it is also enough time to have perspective on a stunning catalog of songs that deserve to live on in a live setting.

I have generally kept my hope for a reunion that will propel the Apples to greater recognition, acknowledgment, and celebration of their cultural significance private from the band, but the thought gives rise to what-ifs.

The Apples in Stereo are more important to indie rock history as a stand-alone band than their Elephant 6 membership card suggests. Robert's reluctance to publicly revisit the era as a source of artistic inspiration is understandable considering all the loss associated with it.

Still, this hasn't kept Robert from acknowledging its impact—not because he seeks recognition; in fact, the reality is seemingly the opposite—but his reticence to return to the kind of songwriting and production that so many would welcome is another loss in and of itself. This feeling is made all the more stark and relevant as Hilarie's frequent releases fronting the High Water Marks consistently remind me of that vintage Apples sound.

"I never thought of doing it, but never say never!" Hilarie says. This response is not related to my personal Apples reunion agenda; it is about the possibility of Hilarie making a solo album under her own name—completely written, engineered, and produced on her own.

Hilarie says she admires Kim Deal of the Pixies, who at sixty-four, has firmly established a legacy for herself and recently released her first solo album under her own name. Similarly, Kim Gordon of Sonic Youth is receiving acclaim throughout the world at seventy-two for her second solo record.

As for my previously mentioned Apples in Stereo reunion agenda, Hilarie is less optimistic.

"I'd do it, but I feel pretty sure that Robert wouldn't," she says. I have asked before and Hilarie has had a similar response before. Frankly, I appreciate that she keeps the what-ifs of my mind from rising too high. Hilarie is a baker (her New York–style bagels look incredibly authentic!), so she knows what happens to bread that overproofs.

Robert's take on where the relationship stands, and how that relates to a potential reunion, may not be as hardened as Hilarie thinks.

"She and I are close, we have been close, we were close as parents, even after we were divorced, and we are still pretty close. So you should know, we are on good terms," Robert says.

"Good terms" is a great place to begin when negotiating personal and professional terms for a reunion tour, or at least some test dates.

When we began discussing this book, I explained to John Hill that I didn't believe the full legacy of the Apples in Stereo had been realized.

"I think there is a level of mystery, especially for much younger people," he says. "We're just so far removed from when we were very active that most people don't even know the extent of how much we actually did."

Is John interested in considering a reunion of some kind, be it a small tour, an album, both, or more?

"If we did that, we could both gauge our legacy as well as define it," he responds.

Eric's recollection of his recent experience of being onstage with Robert and John again at Will's memorial makes it sound like he would be open to the possibilities.

"Nothing brings me greater joy," he says. "It felt great! Since it has been so long, it reverberated more. We have a specific feeling and sound that is different from anyone I've played with before or since."

"Our band was a team, despite whatever 'Brian Wilson–mad genius' archetype that people want to impose on me," Robert explains. "We were a rock band in the traditional sense, but one who had their own studio and label and collective and didn't need the music industry, but still played with it for fun."

Initially, we subconsciously relate to an artist by instinctually expecting the voice coming out of the singer we see to help make sense of the song we hear being sung. Sometimes—and specifically with the artists discussed in this book that are so entrenched and entwined by Elephant 6, their self-made niche in the rock 'n' roll myth—we unintentionally compartmentalize their work.

Jeff Mangum (Neutral Milk Hotel) as sort of the spindly, brooding Syd Barrett–ish reclusive singer-songwriter; Will Hart (the Olivia Tremor Control) as sort of the Daniel Johnston–ish potentially on-the-edge-of-madness multidisciplinarian; and Robert Schneider (the Apples in Stereo) as the joyful, jubilant Brian Wilson–ish crunchy pop guy who also crunches numbers.

Unfortunately, even this mostly subconscious stereotype applied to the Apples disallows the listener to immediately perceive the undercurrent of substance that permeates the band's incredible catalog of songs. The Apples have always been and are always going to be "all three."

In the current phase of his life as a college-level mathematics professor, Robert impresses me as a more authentic version of himself than I knew in our twenties when he was "the Apples in Stereo guy," who also seemed to be burdened on some level with feeling the need to help fulfill the dreams of others.

He seems to have found relief during his continuing journey into numbers, and I hope his love of real numbers will lead him back to writing more musical numbers.

Robert seems whole.

Thank you for indulging my final pun!

"When you cut tape and paste it back together," Robert explained to *Tape Op* in 2018, "the magnetic particles are literally reaching across the gap where the tape was.

"It's meant to mend itself, just like your skin mends itself when you get cut. We're not talking about just cutting something and it's done. We're talking about putting something together and it heals.

"You can hear that."

ACKNOWLEDGMENTS

Friends, Family, and Friends who Feel like Family: Adam Barta, Andrew Murphy, Ben Bloom and the Bloom Family, Bridget Boyd, Colleen Cody, Danny Oppenheim, David, Carrie, and Nova Mikelsons, Colby Brumit, Francesca de Josia, Frank Jaffe, Heidi Anne-Noel, Howard Sage and the Sage Family, James and Leah Toth, Jared Nissim, J.C. Gabel, Jeff Weissler, Leland Pinkham, Phil DeJean, Ricky Yurewich, Roman Stepanov, Rowan Boyd, Sara Tea, Scott Terry and Jenna Pace, Stella the Cat

R.I.P. Aunt Carolee

Professionals, Places, and Professionals at the Places: Adam Clair, Annie Zaleski, Chad Stockfleth, Dan Efram, Danny Goldberg, Ever Kipp, Inara George, Jeff Gomez at J-Card, Mark Bryan, Mark Pellington, Maura Johnston, Mitch Mosk at *Atwood Magazine*

Cathy at Panera, Faith and Cole, and everyone at the Black Cow Coffee Company, Randy and Ethan, and everyone at the Peekskill Coffee House

Lastly, thank you to the Apple core, all Apples past, present, and future, and the extended Apples family!

Robert Schneider, Hilarie Sidney, John Hill, and Eric Allen: You all gave me time to discuss whatever I felt like discussing. Thank you. Frankly, if I were in your shoes, I am not so sure I would want to keep revisiting what I was doing thirty years ago.

It must feel weird when a segment of society is curious about what amounts to a fraction of your life, but that's what happens when you make art that lasts. I'm grateful that you didn't shy away from its greatness when I decided to point out how great it is.

CHAPTER NOTES

1. Hearing the Songs over the Sound of the Scene: Robert Had Too Much to Do!
Peisner, David. "Apples in Stereo's Robert Schneider Gave Up a Flourishing Music Career to Chase His True Passion: Math." *Atlanta*, February 22, 2018. https://www.atlantamagazine.com/great-reads/apples-stereos-robert-schneider-gave-flourishing-music-career-chase-true-passion-math.

2. The Name of This Band Is?
Braud, Ginny. "Incredible Edible Bands: 10 Musical Acts with Munchie Monikers." *Houston Press*, October 18, 2011. https://www.houstonpress.com/restaurants/incredible-edible-bands-10-musical-acts-with-munchie-monikers-6422406.

Gebroe, Dave. "Episode 187. Robert Schneider from the Apples in Stereo: The Discograffiti Interview." *Discograffiti*. December 27, 2024. https://discograffiti.com/podcast/187-robert-schneider-from-the-apples-in-stereo-the-discograffiti-interview.

Clair, Adam. *Endless Endless: A Lo-Fi History of the Elephant 6 Mystery.* New York: Hachette Books, 2022.

3. The Apple in Mono: "I Am Filled with Fire"
Peisner, David. "Apples in Stereo's Robert Schneider Gave Up a Flourishing Music Career to Chase His True Passion: Math." *Atlanta*, February 22, 2018. https://www.atlantamagazine.com/great-reads/apples-stereos-robert-schneider-gave-flourishing-music-career-chase-true-passion-math.

Clair, Adam. *Endless Endless: A Lo-Fi History of the Elephant 6 Mystery.* New York: Hachette Books, 2022.

Waters, Christopher. "Neutral Milk Hotel: Endless Possibilities." *Exclaim!* 1998.

Cooper, Kim. *Neutral Milk Hotel's In the Aeroplane Over the Sea.* London: Bloomsbury Press, 2005.

4. Pet Sounds, Pts. One & Two
Crane, Larry. "Robert Schneider: A Live Interview." *Tape Op.* April 14, 2018. https://tapeop.com/interviews/155/robert-schneider.

Crane, Larry. "The Apples in Stereo: Record Psychedelic Pop in Their Friend's Living Room." *Tape Op.* September 1996. https://tapeop.com/interviews/2/apples-stereo.

5. "All Three": The Songwriting of the Apples in Stereo
Clair, Adam. *Endless Endless: A Lo-Fi History of the Elephant 6 Mystery.* New York: Hachette Books, 2022.

6. Strictly Known as Fuzz and PRE: John Hill & Eric Allen
Clair, Adam. *Endless Endless: A Lo-Fi History of the Elephant 6 Mystery.* New York: Hachette Books, 2022.

Azulai, Noa. "She's the Man Is the Most Important Soccer Movie of All Time." *Vice.* July 11, 2018. https://www.vice.com/en/article/shes-the-man-best-soccer-movie-ever.

7. "Make Sure Everyone Knows Your Contributions": Hilarie Sidney
Marchese, David. "Jann Wenner Defends His Legacy, and His Generation's." *New York Times.* September 15, 2023. https://www.nytimes.com/2023/09/15/arts/jann-wenner-the-masters-interview.html.

Hernandez, Joe. "*Rolling Stone* Founder Jann Wenner Under Fire for Comments on Female, Black Rockers." *NPR*, September 17, 2023. https://www.npr.org/2023/09/17/1200045253/rolling-stone-founder-jann-wenner-under-fire-for-comments-on-female-black-rocker.

O'Hara, Gail. "Hilarie Sidney in Conversation with Jennifer Baron." *Chickfactor Zine.* March 4, 2024. https://www.chickfactor.com/hilarie-sidney-in-conversation-with-jennifer-baron.

Clair, Adam. *Endless Endless: A Lo-Fi History of the Elephant 6 Mystery*. New York: Hachette Books, 2022.

8. Grabbing at the Ring: "Pepsi was our choice, photos were not!"
Clair, Adam. *Endless Endless: A Lo-Fi History of the Elephant 6 Mystery*. New York: Hachette Books, 2022.

Crane, Larry. "Robert Schneider: A Live Interview." *Tape Op*. April 14, 2018. https://tapeop.com/interviews/155/robert-schneider.

Fischer, Tobias. "Hilarie Sidney Shares Her Creative Process." *Fifteen Questions*. September 2023. https://www.15questions.net/interview/hilarie-sidney-apples-stereo-secret-square-high-water-marks-shares-her-creative-process/page-1.

9. What's It Going to Take to Get You into *New Magnetic Wonder* Today?
Cooper, Kim. *Neutral Milk Hotel's In the Aeroplane Over the Sea*. London: Bloomsbury Press, 2005.

Hoard, Christian. "Apples in Stereo Return to Rock." *NPR*. February 6, 2007. https://www.npr.org/2007/02/06/7217587/apples-in-stereo-return-to-rock.

Hoard, Christian. "The Apples in Stereo *New Magnetic Wonder*." *Rolling Stone*. March 7, 2007. http://www.rollingstone.com/reviews/album/13305002/review/13712861/new_magnetic_wonder.

Thompson, Paul. "The Apples in Stereo *Travellers in Space and Time*." *Pitchfork*. April 22, 2010. https://pitchfork.com/reviews/albums/14148-travellers-in-space-and-time.

10. Post-Conceived Bias: "Let Me Tell You 'bout the End of the Beginning"
Crane, Larry. "Robert Schneider: A Live Interview." *Tape Op*, April 14, 2018. https://tapeop.com/interviews/155/robert-schneider.